CW00666216

PHOTOGRAPHERS' LONDON
1839 – 1994

PHOTOGRAPHERS' LONDON
1839–1994

Mike Seaborne

museum of
LONDON

FOR JAN, BEN AND RUTH

First published in Great Britain in 1995 by the Museum of London, 150 London Wall, London EC2Y 5HN

ISBN 0 904818 50 0

Project Manager Suzie Burt
Editorial Suzie Burt, Mandi Gomez, Liz Harrap, Eve Hostettler, Doreen Palamartschuk
Designer Donna Hughes
Photographer Torla Evans
Indexer Diane Russell

Printed and bound by Snoeck-Ducaju & Zoon, Belgium

ACKNOWLEDGEMENTS

D URING the selection of these photographs I have benefited greatly from the guidance of staff at the various museums, archives and picture libraries which have allowed me to reproduce images from their collections. In particular, I would like to thank: Debbie Ireland of the Royal Photographic Society; Ian Leith of the National Buildings Record; Roger Taylor of the National Museum of Photography, Film and Television; Mark Haworth-Booth of the Victoria & Albert Museum; Christopher Denvir of the Greater London Photograph Library; Ralph Hyde and John Fisher of the Guildhall Library, Corporation of London; Bob Aspinall of the Port of London Authority Collection; Thea Duyker of the International Institute for Social History, Amsterdam; Heather Vickers and Annie Chettleborough of Magnum Photos.

I am greatly indebted to John Benton-Harris for allowing me to reproduce prints from his private collection, to David Allison for giving me access to his research notes on George Reid, and to Dorothy Bohm for providing information about Hans Casparious. Special thanks are due to Dan Powell for his invaluable assistance with the biographical research, and to Eve Hostettler for her encouragement and help in the preparation of this book.

Finally, and most importantly, I would like to thank those photographers who have enriched our lives with their unique interpretations of London and its people. They have made the task of selection very difficult. However, it has also been enormously enjoyable.

CONTENTS

FOREWORD BY COLIN OSMAN   8

INTRODUCTION   10

PART ONE

   London and Photography   15

PART TWO

   1839 – 1869   33

   1870 – 1899   59

   1900 – 1918   85

   1919 – 1939   117

   1940 – 1945   165

   1946 – 1969   187

   1970 – 1994   227

APPENDICES

   List of Photographers   288

   List of Illustrations and Acknowledgements   290

   Select Bibliography   294

   Index   296

FOREWORD

THE photographs in this book have been chosen by Mike Seaborne, who is himself a photographer. For this the reader should be profoundly grateful because as a photographer, Mike Seaborne responds to good images, rather than to famous names. Some photographers obviously earned their reputation because of their skill and sensitivity with a camera, but many came to prominence because of their business acumen and their skill at self-promotion. This is as true today as it was in the earliest days of photography and who better to guide the reader through the maze than another photographer?

Mike Seaborne is also curator of the photographic archive at the Museum of London and, of necessity, the historian of that collection. This has given him unique access to the older images, while his personal photography has kept him abreast of modern work. His selection of images, therefore, gives the reader the best of both worlds, and is at once informed and sympathetic.

Photography began in 1839 with three contestants for the first to fix a likeness: Daguerre in Paris, Niepce in Beaune and Talbot in Lacock, Wiltshire. All many miles from London and yet, within two decades, London was to become a world centre of photography.

Britain's first professional studio was opened in Regent Street by Richard Beard, who specialised in making portrait daguerreotypes. Daguerreotypes gave way to processes using negatives and portrait photography boomed in the capital with the mass production of *cartes de visite,* miniature portraits so-called because they were approximately the same size as traditional visiting cards. As techniques developed, the *cartes* were followed by the larger 'Cabinet' portraits and by the growth of landscape photography.

The photographic studios were supported by numerous processing and manufacturing firms in and around London. An early example was Taylor's at Forest Hill, which had a daily output of 1,400 *cartes*, 400 whole-plate prints and sixty enlargements. The list included Harman of Ilford, later to become Ilford of Ilford, matched by Barnet of Barnet. Kodak of Harrow was a relatively latecomer on the scene, but like all manufacturers they had showrooms in central London.

London in the 1880s and 1890s was the portrait and apparatus capital of Britain. It was also the place where photography as art was recognised and displayed. Prints by famous photographers were sold in Bond Street art galleries; their exhibitions, and those of the Royal Photographic Society, were primary outlets for artistic photography.

When snapshot photography arrived many studios closed or became camera equipment, developing and printing shops. The professional portrait gave way to the family snapshot. However, London remained a magnet to photographers from Britain and abroad, both as a place to see and display the best images, and as a place where those images might be created.

The early decades of the twentieth century witnessed the arrival in London of European photographers, many of them refugees from the break-up of the Austro-Hungarian Empire after the First World War and later from the oppression of Nazi Germany. They roamed the streets of the capital with the enthusiasm of outsiders, using the freedom that photojournalism gave to explore and record, not only the streets, but also the people of London.

The Documentary movement in Britain in the 1930s was shaped by international developments, including Soviet communism and the financial depression in the West. The effect was to be seen in both film and still documentary photography, and in the new style of portraiture, a cross between snapshot immediacy and documentary realism. This new approach is exemplified in the work of Cyril Arapoff, Felix Man and Wolfgang Suschitzky.

The end of the Second World War meant the end of the European exodus. In the pôst-War euphoria the urgency of social realism in documentary photography faded away and many of the photographs of the late 1940s and early 1950s look backward, rather than forward. Other forces were at work, led by Tom Hopkinson, editor of *Picture Post*, and Norman Hall, editor of *Photography* magazine. Both were London-based, but international in outlook, and both showed photographs of real merit. Their example was all important

in the days before schools, colleges and galleries of photography. By the mid-1960s, a further change of direction had become apparent, with new influences emanating from the USA, and particularly from New York State and California.

The turning point had probably been the war in Korea, with US forces representing the United Nations (UN). The dramatic demonstration of the role of photography in world politics came with the suppression, by the owner of *Picture Post*, of Bert Hardy's pictures of UN prisoners and the subsequent sacking of the editor Tom Hopkinson. This incident happened in London but the disillusion over the muddled objectives of the war was more strongly felt in America, particularly among the student population (including photography students) and their teachers.

The disillusion was far greater over the Vietnam war, of course, but by then there was a new level of eloquence among photographers. Social documentary increasingly became social criticism, and this was to spread to Europe and beyond.

The photographs of Tony Ray-Jones, and some of those by Ian Berry and John Benton-Harris, are striking images because of their formal qualities, but the photographer, while still often sympathetic, is outside the frame looking in. Ed Barber and Magda Segal are not hostile to their subjects but they are confrontational. The work of David Trainer has an alienated quality typical of this style, and it is also found in the work of Jim Rice and Paul Trevor, but here the directness is coupled with a higher level of information. The pictures by Paul Barkshire and Mike Seaborne abound in information. If there is any hostility, it is towards the system, not individuals. Few would deny that London, like most great cities is in crisis. If we, and I speak as a Cockney, are to find our way through this crisis, it must be by looking at the systems.

Colin Osman, May 1995

9

INTRODUCTION

I wonder if anyone could ever succeed in photographing London? There are the well-known views bought by the hundreds – Trafalgar Square and Piccadilly Circus, the British Museum and Buckingham Palace, Whitehall and Regent Street. But these are not London, any more than a casserole is the same thing as the smells and savours of the dish within. London is something too complex to be caught within a set of views or by any one photographer.

Bill Brandt (1948)

S INCE the invention of photography, photographers have been drawn to London to record and interpret the changing fabric of the capital, the rich diversity of its everyday life and the drama of its epic moments. The result is a tremendous wealth of images housed in public and private collections, including many pictures of exceptional documentary value and photographic quality.

This book contains my personal selection of photographs of London covering the first 155 years of photography, from 1839 to 1994. The pictures are arranged by period and by photographer, with notes on both the photographers and the subject-matter, and they represent a view of the development of photography as it relates to the documentation of London. The majority of the photographs are from the Historic Photographs Collection of the Museum of London. The remainder are mostly from other public collections or from the photographers themselves.

The hundreds of thousands of images which are available made the selection of photographs extremely difficult. Interior views and studio portraits have been excluded, for the most part, in favour of photographs which reflect a sense of place. I have sought to show the ways in which London has been interpreted by different photographers at different times, and if there is a conscious bias in the selection it is towards the work of those photographers, whether amateur or professional, who have responded to London on a personal level.

It has been said that there are no great photographers only great photographs, and each picture in this book has been chosen on its own merits, not the fame of its creator. As one of the world's greatest cities, London has of course attracted the attention of some very well-known photographers and examples of the work of several of them are included here. There are, however, many fine images by other, less celebrated, photographers and these are given equal pride of place. One of the most exciting consequences of researching this book was the discovery of many wonderful photographs which have never, as far as I am aware, been published before, and I am delighted to be able to include some of these too.

Although the book is not intended to be a history of modern London, or a history of photography, it does contain material relevant to an understanding of both. There will, inevitably, be those who come to this book hoping to find particular photographs of London or work by certain photographers, and who will be disappointed at not finding them. To them I can only extend my apologies. I would have liked to have included many more images but this would have made the book simply too big.

The photographic record of London presented here necessarily reflects the concerns and interests of its creators and there are many gaps in it which have arisen for one reason or another. Some of these are quite general, for instance in recording the fabric of London there has always been an emphasis on buildings in the centre rather than those in the suburbs, and as far as the social record is concerned there are many more documentary photographs of working-class people than there are of those from other social groups.

Some omissions are more specific and relate either to the state of photographic technology at the time or to prevailing cultural and social values or to both. For example, 'instantaneous' photographs of moving objects, such as traffic and people in the street, do not exist before the early 1860s because the available photographic materials were too insensitive to capture motion. On the other hand in the late 1980s and early 1990s, and despite the greatly increased speed of photographic film and equipment, there was a similar paucity of candid street photography, but due this time, apparently, to a lack of motivation by photographers.

If change in relation to developing photographic technology, choice of subject-matter and approach are themes which emerge from a study of London's photographic record, another is continuity in terms of the enduring nature of certain photographic practices. There is, for example, much similarity in technique and intent between some photographers recording new buildings in London in the 1860s and 1870s and those doing the same thing in the 1980s and 1990s. Both groups used large-format equipment to give maximum image control and descriptive quality, and had a common desire to record the new buildings in relation to the existing built environment.

The photographs on the following pages are offered as personal views of London and its people and as examples of photographic art. Whatever the intentions of their creators, photographs are always incomplete or partial representations of visible reality and can sometimes seriously mislead if taken purely at face value. Bill Brandt's words remind us of the unfathomable complexity of London's character, and our ability to understand it is perhaps as much challenged as it is helped by the variety of images provided by its equally varied photographers.

Mike Seaborne, March 1995

PART ONE

LONDON AND PHOTOGRAPHY

16

THE FIRST PHOTOGRAPHS OF LONDON

T HE first public announcement of the invention of photography was made in January 1839, and in September or October of that year the first photographs of London were taken. These early images are daguerreotypes made by the Frenchman, **Monsieur de St. Croix (opposite, above left)**, and were taken in the vicinity of Trafalgar Square. Few later daguerreotypes of London survive, and it may be that not very many were taken because the process was patented in England and a licence to use it was prohibitively expensive.

A rival photographic process, the calotype, was introduced in 1841 by the Englishman, **William Henry Fox Talbot (opposite, below left)**. Unlike the daguerreotype, which was a one-off positive image on a silvered metal plate, the calotype was a paper negative from which many positive prints on salt paper could be made. Use of the calotype process in England was also limited by patent restrictions, so not many people could use that either, at least not professionally. Talbot, however, took quite a few photographs of London himself during the 1840s and copies of many of these survive. They are mainly architectural views and often show new or refurbished buildings. Talbot must have thought that there would be a demand for his pictures because he set up a printing works in Reading in 1843 to mass-produce salt prints from his own negatives and those of others, and these were sold through a shop in London. However, the printing works closed in 1847, to be followed by the failure and closure of the shop, so perhaps there was not yet a commercially viable market for such photographic views.

THE WET-PLATE ERA

In the early 1850s, photography was given an enormous boost by the invention of the wet collodion process. As well as being relatively fast, this was free from patent restrictions and so was available to all who could afford the materials. Also, as the negative was on glass rather than on paper, the definition of the picture was a great deal higher. Most photography before 1860 was undertaken in the studio, where the taking of portraits, especially *cartes de visite*, was good business, but a number of photographers specialised in the making of views. Many of these were well-off amateurs who did not seek financial gain, people like Count de Montizon, Roger Fenton and **George Shadbolt (opposite, above right)**. They photographed in London in the 1850s and were among those responsible for setting up the Photographic Society in 1853.

New camera and lens designs meant that photographic exposure times had become so short by the early 1860s that the photographer **Valentine Blanchard (opposite, below right)** was able to take the first 'instantaneous' photographs in London's busy streets, rendering moving people and objects in sharp focus. The value of photography as a recording medium was also becoming increasingly important at a time when Victorian engineers and builders, such as William Cubitt, Isambard Kingdom Brunel and Joshua Bazelgette, were carrying out major infrastructure and redevelopment works. During the 1860s and 1870s in particular, much of the London which could by the end of the nineteenth century be called 'the capital of the greatest empire the world has ever known', was being created. At the same time many buildings which had survived from the seventeenth and eighteenth centuries were threatened with demolition. Henry Flather and Henry Dixon, for example, were commissioned to record the progress of large engineering projects, especially those related to the new road and railway networks, whilst William Strudwick and John Sanford photographed streets and buildings which were to be demolished. Strudwick's work in particular deserves close attention because although some of his photographs have been widely reproduced, they have rarely been correctly attributed. Strudwick's contribution to the early photography of London remains to be fully assessed, but it would seem that it was much greater than has so far been realised.

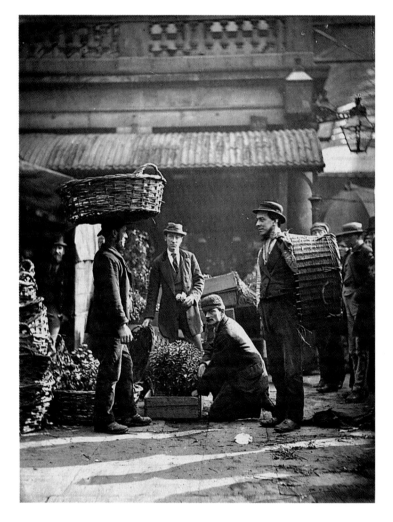

THE FIRST SOCIAL DOCUMENTARY PHOTOGRAPHY

STRUDWICK and Sanford were followed in the mid-1870s by Alfred and John Bool who photographed similar (and sometimes the same) subjects, this time on behalf of the Society for Photographing Relics of Old London. In the 1880s **Henry Dixon (opposite, above left)** was commissioned to take further photographs of historic buildings for the Society.

The first real photographic social documentary project to be carried out in London was undertaken by **John Thomson (opposite, below right)** who produced a series of semi-formal environmental portraits of various street characters, published as a part-work, *Street Life in London*, in 1877–1878. The photographs were reproduced together with essays based on interviews with those depicted, written by Adolphe Smith, a writer and political activist, or occasionally by Thomson himself. The concept was not entirely new, because in the 1840s Henry Mayhew had published the results of a larger investigation into London's street life, also based on interviews, which was illustrated by engravings copied from daguerreotypes taken by Richard Beard. Thomson and Smith acknowledged Mayhew's work but justified their own efforts in terms of providing an up-to-date picture and using actual photographs to counter any accusations of having exaggerated the physical characteristics of their subjects. *Street Life in London* was the first example of what was to become an extremely important area of photographic practice.

GELATINE DRY PLATES AND HAND CAMERAS

A new era in photography began when fast, reliable dry plates became commercially available in the 1880s. The whole process became much simpler and cheaper and the number of professional photographers increased dramatically. Photographic views had became very popular by this time and the market for these was large enough to support several specialist firms, most of whom had a stock of views of London. Some of the best views of London were made by George Washington Wilson and his son,

Charles, and other striking images were produced by firms such as the London Stereoscopic and Photographic Company and Francis G.O. Stuart.

The hand-held camera was also developed at around this time, enabling snapshot photography to come into being. One of the earliest serious users of the hand camera was **Paul Martin (opposite, below left)** who photographed extensively in London's streets in the early 1890s with a detective camera, catching his subjects completely unawares. This work marked the beginning of candid street photography in England, although at the time, Martin's snapshots were not highly regarded.

The success of the Eastman Kodak Co., which in 1888 launched its first camera with the slogan, 'You press the button, we do the rest', signalled the rise of photography as a popular pastime. Few amateur 'snappers' of the period produced pictures of London of any great significance, but some of the cameras made by Kodak were capable of yielding excellent results in the right hands. George Davison, Managing Director of Kodak Ltd, was an influential amateur photographer who took one of the newly-introduced Kodak swing-lens panoramic cameras into the streets of London in around 1900, producing some interesting images.

PICTORIALISM

A T the turn of the century, groups of photographers in Britain and America, influenced by the Impressionist movement in painting, began to develop an aesthetic in photography designed to establish once and for all the status of the medium as an art form. A number of the leading figures took photographs in London, including Walter Benington, Charles Job and the American, **Alvin Langdon Coburn (opposite, above left)**. The work of these and other pictorialists was characterised by carefully controlled composition, an emphasis on conveying atmosphere rather than the rendering of fine detail, and the hand-working of the final print to create a painterly effect. The Thames, with its reflective surface, its romantic associations and the wonderful shapes and patterns of its boats and bridges, was a particularly favoured London subject.

THE PUBLIC RECORD

Political and social reforms at the end of the nineteenth century, notably the Local Government Act of 1888, led to the establishment of new regional and local authorities and the creation of new public services, or the expansion of existing ones. Foremost amongst these new bodies in London was the London County Council (LCC), which was established by the 1888 Act. This and other authorities began to commission photographers to record their activities or the progress of their works, and in a number of instances these photographs have come to form the basis of major public collections, such as the Greater London Photographs Library and the Photographic Collection of the City of London Guildhall Library. As well as the LCC, both Westminster City Council and the Port of London Authority, established in 1909, began to commission photography at this time. The photographer, **John H. Avery (opposite, above right)**, was a major figure in this field, carrying out high-quality work for all three of these organisations. Other bodies concerned with the physical, social or spiritual condition of Londoners also used photography to further their aims. The Church and some evangelical groups,

such as the London City Mission, recognised the power of photography in documenting the plight of those whom they believed needed their help, and used photographs to illustrate public lectures about their work. In the case of the London City Mission it was one of their own missionaries, the **Rev. John Galt (opposite, below left)**, who took the photographs to accompany his lectures.

PHOTOGRAPHY AND THE PRINTED PAGE

By the end of the nineteenth century it had become possible to print photographs alongside text in books, magazines and newspapers on a commercial scale. Publications such as the *Illustrated London News* had been using photographs as the basis for illustrations long before this, but only for copy as woodcuts, not as half-tones. Several photographically-illustrated books on London appeared before the First World War and many more were printed in the 1920s and 1930s. A particularly prolific illustrator of books about London was the German-born photographer, Emil Otto Hoppé, who had published at least four by the mid-1930s. George Reid had an ambitious idea for a book of London photographs, and although his untimely death in 1933 meant that the book itself never materialised, he produced a superb set of street and river views. The East End portrait photographer, William Whiffin, also photographed in various parts of London, and a number of his pictures were used in a particularly well-illustrated three-volume publication, *Wonderful London*, published in 1927. The first photographic press agency was established in London in 1894 and in 1904 the *Daily Mirror* became the first national newspaper to be illustrated entirely with photographs. One of the earliest press photographers in London was **Horace Nicholls (opposite, below right)** who worked there as a freelancer from about 1900, after making his reputation photographing the Boer War. Another press photographer of note was James Jarché whose career spanned many decades and who also achieved some recognition for his work. Most press photographers, however, remained entirely anonymous, their work only being credited to the agency which employed them. One agency which produced excellent photographs on various London subjects in the late 1920s and 1930s was Fox Photos.

PHOTO-REPORTAGE

T HE early 1930s saw the emergence in Britain of a new kind of photography, which its practitioners called 'photo-reportage'. These photographers were mostly well-educated émigrés from Germany who left after Adolf Hitler was elected Chancellor in 1933. They brought with them the experience of producing photographic stories for popular German illustrated magazines which they had themselves researched, photographed and written. Britain's first magazine based on the continental model, *Weekly Illustrated*, was established in London in 1934 under the direction of Stefan Lorant, a Hungarian who had worked in Germany before being arrested and deported by the Nazis in 1933.

The technique of most photo-reporters involved the use of the recently introduced 'miniature' hand-held rollfilm cameras, such as the Rollieflex, Leica, and Contax. These were unobtrusive, speedy in operation and enabled sequences of closely-timed photographs to be taken without having to reload with film. One of the most prominent of the German émigré photo-reporters was **Felix H. Man (opposite, above left)** who photographed a number of stories about London for *Weekly Illustrated*. He was subsequently involved with Lorant in setting up a new magazine, *Picture Post*, which first appeared in 1938. This highly-regarded magazine was one of the best of its kind anywhere in the world and did more than any other publication to develop British photojournalism. It pioneered, amongst other things, the 'day in the life' approach and published many photographic stories concerned with London.

Another German-born photographer who worked for both *Weekly Illustrated* and *Picture Post* was **Bill Brandt (opposite, below right)**, whose documentary work included the production of photo-stories for magazines. **Cyril Arapoff (opposite, below left)**, a Russian who photographed London in the 1930s, also embraced photo-reportage techniques, but like Brandt, he had a wider interest in photography as a documentary medium, and his work was often featured in the photographic press. Other photographers engaged in documenting aspects of London at this time included Humphrey Spender and Margaret Monck, who were also early users of miniature cameras. In 1937 the French master of miniature camera technique, Henri Cartier-Bresson, came to London to photograph the Coronation of George VI.

24

PHOTOGRAPHY AND THE LONDON BLITZ

T HE period from September 1940 to May 1941 was the most momentous in London's recent history. Usually referred to as the 'London Blitz', the devastation and social upheaval caused by the incessant German bombing was an obvious subject for photographic documentation, but such photography was kept within carefully prescribed limits by wartime restrictions.

To take photographs of anything even remotely connected with the War, a photographer had to obtain appropriate accreditation, usually from a newspaper or press agency, before applying for a photographic permit. All photographs taken by authorised photographers had to be submitted to the official Censor before they could be published or distributed. Speed is of the essence in reporting current events, and the last thing an editor wants is a delay in receiving photographs passed for publication. As a result, wartime press photographers were under pressure only to take pictures of an uncontroversial nature. Of equal significance, however, was the attitude of the general public towards War reporting. There was a widely-held belief in the need to promote national unity and to maintain morale in the fight against Hitler. Therefore, photographers, along with everybody else, willingly practised self-censorship in the interests of showing the rest of the world that 'Britain can take it'.

Amongst the many thousands of photographs of wartime London there are some which are of particular interest. These include the work of **George Rodger (opposite, below right)**, who was working as a London-based freelancer for the American *Life* magazine, and **Bert Hardy (opposite, above left)**, who photographed several stories of the London Blitz for *Picture Post*. The latter magazine achieved great popularity during the War, not least because it reflected public opinion closely and was at times critical of the government's handling of the War effort. A small number of anonymous press agency photographs also stand out as memorable images.

Of special interest, too, are some of the photographs taken purely for record purposes. These include the photographs of bomb damage in the City taken by **Arthur Cross and Fred Tibbs (opposite, below left)** for the City of London police files, and the official Home Office record of conditions in some of the underground shelters which was made by Bill Brandt and another photographer whose identity does not seem to have been recorded. Photographs like these are very different from the stereotypical flag-waving images often published in the press, and serve to highlight the bias of the photographic process.

PHOTOGRAPHY IN POST-WAR LONDON

ILLUSTRATED newspapers and magazines thrived in the 1940s and 1950s, thus enabling pre-War photo-reportage to mature into post-War photojournalism. Until it closed in 1957, *Picture Post* continued to be the leading vehicle in Britain for photo-stories, and several of these were concerned with London, giving scope for photojournalists like Bert Hardy and Thurston Hopkins to show their abilities. Humanist in tone, the stories covered a wide range of issues from serious social concerns of the day to more light-hearted matters. *Picture Post's* social commitment seemed to wane after Tom Harrison, its editor from 1940, was sacked in 1950 over an argument with the proprietor about the use of a report on the American army's treatment of political prisoners during the Korean War. By the end of the 1950s the demand for magazines devoted to photo-stories was beginning to decline as television started to compete for public attention.

During the 1950s, a new kind of documentary photographer had begun to emerge, concerned with carrying out more extensive and personal photographic investigations than were appropriate for a magazine article. This development was most marked in America, but one British pioneer of this approach was **Roger Mayne (opposite, above left)**, who worked on a project documenting street life in London's North Kensington over a period of several years. At this time, too, a number of continental photographers visited London, including Henri Cartier-Bresson. As an independent photojournalist with the agency Magnum Photos, which he co-founded in 1947 with George Rodger, Robert Capa and David Seymour, Cartier-Bresson made a number of outstanding photographs in London during the 1950s. Several photographic books on London appeared, including *Gala Day London* by Izis Bidermanas (1953), and *The Living City* by Edwin Smith (1957), both largely celebratory in character and showing something of everyday life in post-War London. Unfortunately, with one or two exceptions, very few good photographs of the rebuilding of London's war-torn streets have come to light.

THE COMMERCIAL 1960s

In the 1960s, photography in Britain was given a boost with the rapid expansion of magazine publication and the introduction of Sunday newspaper colour supplements containing photographic features. However, at a time when consumer interests were moving to the top of the media agenda, the new photographic opportunities lay more in the worlds of advertising and fashion than they did in documentary photography. Serious photographers *of* London, as opposed to those who were simply working *in* London, were apparently few and far between.

Some of the best documentary photographs of London in this period were made either by foreign visitors such as the American, **Jerome Liebling (opposite, above left)**, or by British photographers working for foreign publications, such as Terry Spencer's work for *Life* magazine. American photographic influences, including the work of Robert Frank, Diane Arbus and Gary Winogrand, were important, but so too was the development of a new cultural climate which led, amongst other things, to the establishment of new academic institutions concerned with promoting social and psychological studies. One of the few significant English documentarists to photograph in London in the 1960s, **Tony Ray-Jones (opposite, right)**, had trained in America, and his work, which is full of sociological and psychological insight, was to prove influential. Sadly, he died of leukemia in 1972 at the age of thirty. His close friend, the American photographer, John Benton-Harris, had settled near London in the early 1960s and subsequently embarked on an extensive photographic study of the English character, much of which, at least until the early 1980s, was carried out in the London area.

A NEW ERA FOR PHOTOGRAPHY

A FULL account of British photography during the 1970s and 1980s remains to be written, but it is possible to say that the early 1970s were something of a watershed. The Photographers' Gallery opened in London in 1971, other photography galleries such as the Half Moon, later Camerawork, in East London, soon followed, and the Arts Council began to provide financial support for photographers to carry out personal work. Documentary photography between the 1930s and 1950s was rediscovered through exhibitions and magazines such as *Creative Camera*. At the same time there was a renewed interest in socially-concerned photography which was allied to a perception of the need to document traditional communities whose continued existence was threatened by contemporary economic forces.

This was also the moment when 'straight' photography started to receive serious attention in some of the major art institutions and photographic studies were added to higher education curricula. It seemed at last that documentary photographers might be accorded the same artistic status as those using photography in other contexts. Of equal significance was the rapidly-growing recognition of the value of photographs as historical evidence and the consequent development of photographic collections by museums and libraries, including the occasional commissioning of independent documentary work. By the end of the 1970s, the principal outlets for creative documentary photography had become the gallery, the art and cultural magazine and the museum archive.

Several documentary photographers were working on personal projects in London in the 1970s. Notable among them are **Paul Trevor (opposite, above left)** and **Jim Rice (opposite, above right)** who are still actively photographing in the 1990s. Trevor's work in particular represents a high level of commitment and dedication to the documentation of one part of London, the area around Brick Lane in the East End, over a period of twenty years.

The Magnum agency photographer, Ian Berry, the first photographer to receive a major Arts Council award, revealed some contrasting aspects of mid-1970s London society as part of an investigation of the English race, published in book-form in 1978, and there were one or two other photographers who published similar studies. Also in 1978, and with the aid of an Arts Council grant, the Museum of London gave its first photographic commission to Barry Lewis to document commuting in London, and in 1979, the Museum appointed the author of this book as the first full-time curator of its Historic Photographs Collection.

QUANTITY AND DIVERSITY

One result of the heightened interest in photography and photographic collecting was that many older, often retired, photographers came to realise that their work might still be of value and so began to offer it to museums and archives. In 1986, for example, the Museum of London acquired the entire collection of black and white photographs of London taken by the freelance photojournalist, Henry Grant, during the 1950s, 1960s and 1970s. At the same time, a large number of talented and eager young documentary photographers, many of them graduates from one of the photography degree or diploma courses, began to come onto the scene.

Established documentary approaches were supplemented in the 1980s by the development of new visual styles based on a re-evaluation of photographic content or on an exploration of the formal possibilities offered by new colour materials, or on both. This included the growing importance of photographic work which dealt with the social and political as well as the personal and formal, content of landscape. This development paralleled environmental studies in other fields. In London, some of the most urgent contemporary issues were those related directly to infrastructure provision and to land-use planning, for example in the Docklands area of the East End, which was then being redeveloped following the closure of the docks. Such environmental concerns were reflected in the work of a number of documentary and landscape photographers, including Peter Marshall, Tom Evans, **Alan Delaney (see page 28, below left)**, and the author.

INTO THE 1990s

Paradoxically, whilst what had became known as the 'independent' sector had expanded and diversified during the 1980s, so the prevailing political ideology forced many ostensibly non-commercial photographers into an ever-increasing reliance on commercial sources for financial support. The number of photographers had grown much more rapidly than the number of real photographic opportunities, leading to a situation where exposure of the latest trend was taking precedence over the showing of less innovative, but possibly more enduring, work. Happily, though, in the early 1990s there were still photographers working in London, and elsewhere, whose ambitions were not circumscribed by such considerations.

At the time of writing, we are firmly in the grip of a digital imaging revolution, which is seen by some as a threat to the continued existence of photography. In this context, the end-piece to this book, **Tom Hunter and James Mackinnon's (see page 28, below right)** photographic model, 'London Fields – The Ghetto', is particularly fitting. Overwhelmingly large, interactive and made using conventional photographic materials, it represents a way of using photographs which enhances their documentary effect. It offers an experience which is much more convincing than anything yet possible in the digital world of virtual reality and suggests that the unique qualities of photography will not be easily simulated by the computer. The innovative approach represented by this and other work leaves me in no doubt that photographers will continue to contribute to the documentary record of London for the forseeable future.

PART TWO

1839 – 1869

ST. CROIX, a Frenchman, has the distinction of having taken the earliest surviving photographs of London. He was also the first to demonstrate the daguerreotype process in England, on 13 September 1839, and during October of that year he arranged exhibitions of daguerreotypes and further demonstrations of the process at the Royal Adelaide Gallery of Practical Science in West Strand. However, at the end of October the English licensee of the process, Miles Berry, took out an injunction against St. Croix which forced him to stop these activities.

M. DE ST. CROIX (ACTIVE 1839)

Whitehall from Trafalgar Square, September/October, 1839

Daguerreotype. Victoria & Albert Museum (1-1986)

The daguerreotype process was capable of recording fine detail, as this earliest surviving photograph of London ably demonstrates. However, because the image was produced as a direct positive, it is reversed left to right. Anything in the scene that moved during the lengthy exposure was not recorded, thus giving the probably false impression that the street was mostly deserted.

A S THE English inventor of the first negative-positive photographic process, the calotype, in 1841, Talbot was quick to test the commercial viability of selling and publishing prints. In 1843 he set up an establishment in Reading, halfway between London and his home at Lacock in Wiltshire, for producing multiple salt prints from calotype negatives. His photographs included many architectural studies and he seems to have concentrated, in London at least, on the recording of buildings which had recently been completed or rebuilt. Commercial interest in photography in the early years was mainly confined to portraiture, however, and Talbot's pioneering venture was not a great success.

WILLIAM HENRY FOX TALBOT [1800–1877]

Trafalgar Square and Nelson's Column, 1843

Salt print from calotype negative. National Museum of Photography, Film & Television (1937-3943)

Printed from a paper calotype negative, the detail of this salt print lacks the definition that a daguerreotype would have had, but the image has the merit of being the right way round and any number of prints could easily be made from a single negative. The subject is a good example of Talbot's interest in photographing new buildings in London and he often chose elevated positions from which to take his pictures. The calotype process, like the daguerreotype, required exposure times too long for movement to be recorded. The picture was taken as the scaffolding was being removed from the newly-erected Nelson's Column.

Hungerford Suspension Bridge, from the North Bank Looking South, c. 1845

Salt print from Calotype negative. National Museum of Photography, Film & Television (1937-3949)

This elegant foot bridge was designed by Isambard Kingdom Brunel, an acquaintance of Talbot, and was built between 1841 and 1845.

KILBURN was a professional photographer who used the daguerreotype process to take studio portraits. In 1847 he became a 'Photographist to Her Majesty and His Royal Highness, Prince Albert'.

WILLIAM KILBURN (ACTIVE 1840s–1860s)

Chartists' Rally, Kennington Common, 10 April 1848

Daguerreotype. Royal Archives, Windsor

This is one of two surviving daguerreotypes of the Chartists' rally which are believed to have been taken by Kilburn. The photographs are remarkable in recording unposed people rather than static objects or buildings, and it is believed that they were taken for police records. The demonstration was held on the Common to coincide with the Chartist leaders' presentation of a petition to Parliament, and a large crowd was expected in support of the campaign to extend democratic rights. In the event, however, the gathering was much smaller than anticipated.

ROSLING was a successful timber merchant in Hackney and an amateur calotypist. He became the first Treasurer of the Photographic Society of London, formed in 1853, and was on the Photographic Committee of the Royal Panoptican of Science and Art.

ALFRED ROSLING (1802 – c. 1882)

The Riverfront and St. Paul's Cathedral from London Bridge, c. 1853

Albumen print from waxed paper negative. Reproduced by Gracious Permission of Her Majesty the Queen

Rosling took this fascinating view of the north bank of the Thames from London Bridge. It shows some of what were once London's principal trading wharves.

IKE many of the pioneers of pictorial photography, Count de Montizon was a wealthy amateur. He was an early member of the Photographic Society of London, founded in 1853, which became the Royal Photographic Society in 1894.

COUNT DE MONTIZON (ACTIVE 1850s)

The Hippopotamus at the Zoological Gardens, Regent's Park, c. 1855

Salt print from wet collodion negative. Royal Photographic Society (11455)

This hippopotamus at Regent's Park Zoo was brought to London from Egypt in 1849. Count de Montizon's photograph of the sleeping animal (the emulsion speed of his wet-plate negative would have been too slow to have recorded the hippo if it was moving) ably captures the sense of spectacle, though it is debatable whether the onlookers are more interested in the animal or in the photographer: they were both rarities in the 1850s.

ANONYMOUS

William Smith, Aged 19, Before Deportation to Canada, c. 1856

Salt print. Guildhall Library, Corporation of London (MSS Department)

This photograph is from a little-known but fascinating album apparently compiled as a record of homeless London youths who were assisted in the furtherance of their careers by being deported to Canada by an unknown agency. Each photograph in the album is accompanied by biographical notes on the young man concerned. William Smith was wounded in the Crimea in 1855 and sent to Canada in 1857.

LITTLE is known about Howlett except that he was commended by Queen Victoria for his portraits of Crimean War heroes in 1856, and was a partner with Joseph Cundall and George Downes at the Photographic Institution in New Bond Street in the late 1850s. In 1857 he photographed the construction of Isambard Kingdom Brunel's ship, 'Great Eastern', probably as a commission from the ship's builder, John Scott Russell & Co. The *Illustrated London News* used some of the photographs as copy for wood engravings.

ROBERT HOWLETT (1831 [?] –1858)

I. K. Brunel by the Launching Chains of the 'Great Eastern', Millwall, Isle of Dogs, November 1857

Albumen print. Institute of Civil Engineers

The 'Great Eastern', built by John Scott Russell & Co., was then the world's largest steamship with an iron hull and represented a triumph of Victorian engineering. However, its development contributed to the decline of shipbuilding on the Thames because the raw materials for smelting iron were not to be found in the London area. Howlett's photographs were taken shortly before the first, unsuccessful, attempt at launching the vessel on 14 November 1857.

Construction of the 'Great Eastern' – side view, Millwall, Isle of Dogs, November 1857

Albumen print. Institute of Civil Engineers

Construction of the 'Great Eastern' – bow-on view, Millwall, Isle of Dogs, November 1857

Albumen print. Institute of Civil Engineers

ENTON is one of the best known nineteenth-century British photographers, especially for his documentary images of the aftermath of the Crimean War, taken in and around Balaclava in 1855. He took up photography in the 1840s after studying Law at University College, London, and painting with the history painter, Charles Lucy. Initially he used the calotype paper negative process, but by 1852 was making large collodion wet-plate negatives. In 1853 he was a founding member of the Photographic Society of London and regularly exhibited at the Society's annual exhibition until 1861. From 1854 to 1858 he worked as photographer to the British Museum, and during this period he completed a series of large-format topographical views of London.

ROGER FENTON (1819–1869)

Buckingham Palace, c. 1857

Salt print from wet collodion negative. Private Collection

Buckingham Palace has been the London home of the monarchy since Victoria became Queen in 1837. It was substantially rebuilt to the designs of John Nash between 1825 and 1837, and a new East Wing, shown here, was added between 1847 and 1850. This hitherto unrecorded photograph is very similar to a published view of the palace, and both were probably taken by Fenton at the same time.

Westminster Abbey and the Palace of Westminster Under Construction, c. 1857

Salt print from wet collodion negative. Private Collection

In the late 1850s Fenton took several photographs to record the construction of the new Palace of Westminster, designed by Charles Barry and Augustus Pugin, which was built to replace the old palace destroyed by fire in 1834. In this previously unpublished view the 336-foot Victoria Tower can be seen in the distance on the right, whilst behind and to the left of the Abbey is the smaller, but more famous Clock Tower which houses the clock and bell named Big Ben.

SHADBOLT had a successful timber business in the City of London and was a keen amateur photographer. He was a founding member of the Photographic Society of London and was editor, from 1857 to 1864, of the *British Journal of Photography*. He lived at Crouch End in the Parish of Hornsey to the north of London, when the area still consisted largely of open countryside. He made a series of landscape views in and around the Vale of Hornsey, perhaps realising that before long it would be swallowed up by the 'march of bricks' out of London.

GEORGE SHADBOLT (1819–1901)

Vale of Hornsey, c. 1860

Salt print. Bruce Castle Museum

Although London was expanding at an enormous rate during the second half of the nineteenth century, few photographers apart from Shadbolt seem to have been interested in recording rural areas like Hornsey before they were built over.

46

ROUT published a series of landscape views of the Thames, titled *The Thames from London to Oxford in Forty Photographs*, in 1862.

VICTOR ALBERT PROUT (ACTIVE 1860s)

Eel Pie Island, c. 1862

Albumen print. Victoria & Albert Museum (129-1987)

BLANCHARD was the first photographer to take his camera onto the busy London streets in order to capture their hustle and bustle. The camera was mounted on the roof of a cab parked in the street and the exposure times were kept as short as possible in order to 'freeze' the movement. These so-called 'instantaneous' photographs were made with a small camera designed to produce a pair of images for viewing in a stereoscope. Photographic stereocards were very popular in the early 1860s and Blanchard found a good market for his pictures. However, by the end of the 1860s stereocards had lost their appeal and so Blanchard switched to portrait photography.

VALENTINE BLANCHARD (1831–1901)

Temple Bar, Fleet Street/Strand, c. 1862

Albumen prints (stereo pair). Museum of London (IN14862)

Temple Bar straddled the road at the meeting point of the Strand and Fleet Street until 1878 when it was removed to facilitate the flow of traffic. It was re-erected some years later in Theobald's Park, Cheshunt, Hertfordshire, where it still stands in 1995.

The River and the Palace of Westminster, c. 1860

Albumen print. Royal Photographic Society (3800/9)

Blanchard photographed the Thames in similar fashion to his 'instantaneous' street pictures, freezing the movement of both vessels and water. This particular location was probably chosen to record the newly-rebuilt Palace of Westminster.

No. 516.—Temple Bar.

PHOTOGRAPHS of manufacturing industry in London before the end of the nineteenth century are few and far between. These rare photographs were taken by seventeen-year-old Geoffrey Bevington, a keen amateur photographer, for display on the firm's stand at the 1862 International Exhibition at the Crystal Palace. The firm's products were highly praised and won several awards.

GEOFFREY BEVINGTON (c.1845–?)

Bevington & Sons Tannery, Neckinger Mills, Bermondsey –
View of the Factory from the Surrey Canal, 1862
Albumen print. Victoria & Albert Museum

Bevington & Sons Tannery, Neckinger Mills, Bermondsey –
'Finishing Skivers and Persians for Hat Linings and Boot Purposes', 1862
Albumen print. Victoria & Albert Museum

FLATHER, a professional photographer based in Regent Street, was commissioned to take a series of progress photographs of the construction of the underground line from South Kensington to Westminster Bridge, which was built between 1865 and 1868. His photographic record included several views of the surface works at different points along the route. These clearly show the 'cut-and-cover' method of construction.

HENRY FLATHER (ACTIVE 1860s – 1870s)

Construction of the Metropolitan District Railway, Sloane Square, c. 1866
Albumen print. Institute of Civil Engineers

Construction of the Metropolitan District Railway, Victoria, c. 1866
Albumen print. Institute of Civil Engineers

THE extent of Strudwick's photographic activity in London in the 1860s and early 1870s has not been fully documented, but the large number of pictures which can be attributed to him in various public collections suggests that it may have been quite considerable. He certainly photographed in many different parts of London, including Westminster, Lambeth, Southwark and the City of London, and his superb architectural and topographical views record the fabric of the city at a time when redevelopment was bringing about great changes to the way London looked. He photographed several historic buildings in the 1860s which were recorded again in the 1870s and 1880s by the Society for Photographing Relics of Old London. The Society used a negative taken by Strudwick to make the carbon prints of the Water Gate of York House which it issued to subscribers in 1882.

WILLIAM STRUDWICK [ACTIVE 1860s – 1870s]

A Riverside View of Houses in Fore Street, Lambeth, c. 1866

Albumen print. Guildhall Library, Corporation of London (St. Paul's Collection)

These houses are clearly slum properties and they may have suffered from the flooding which occurred regularly along this part of the Thames. They were demolished to make way for the Albert Embankment, the construction of which started in 1866.

Statue of Richard I, Old Palace Yard, Westminster, c. 1865

Albumen print. Victoria & Albert Museum (59-408)

This superb picture of Carlo Marochetti's bronze statue is one of several photographs which Strudwick took in and around the Palace of Westminster shortly after it was completed in the early 1860s. Strudwick was a professional photographer and so it must be assumed that he was either commissioned to record views such as this or that there was a market for his prints. It is known that the South Kensington Museum's Department of Science and Art purchased many prints from Strudwick, including this one, in 1868–1869.

New Street or Princes Street, Lambeth, c. 1866

Albumen print. Guildhall Library, Corporation of London (St. Paul's Collection)

Strudwick took several photographs of streets and industrial premises near the Lambeth riverside.

Old Houses, Holborn Bars, c. 1868

Albumen print. Guildhall Library, Corporation of London (St. Paul's Collection)

These houses, which still stand, form part of Staple Inn and may date from the late sixteenth century. In 1911 they were restored and painted in black and white, as was then thought appropriate for timber and frame buildings. Strudwick took this photograph at least ten years before Alfred and John Bool recorded it for the Society for Photographing Relics of Old London in 1878.

View Across Queen Victoria Street Towards St. Paul's Cathedral, c. 1870

Albumen print. Guildhall Library, Corporation of London (St. Paul's Collection)

The photograph appears to have been taken during the latter stages of the construction of Queen Victoria Street, which was opened in 1871. The tower of St. Andrew-by-the Wardrobe, on the right, was in the process of being remodelled.

DIXON was commissioned by the Corporation of London in 1869 to record the progress of the building of Holborn Viaduct, and in the late 1870s he was engaged by the Society for Photographing Relics of Old London to photograph historic buildings threatened with demolition. Dixon printed his photographs, and those taken earlier for the Society by Alfred and John Bool, in the permanent carbon process, and they were issued to subscribers together with printed notes on the histories of the buildings depicted. *See also pages 70–2.*

HENRY DIXON (1820–1893)

Panorama of Holborn Viaduct Under Construction, 1869

Albumen prints (three), Guildhall Library, Corporation of London
(Pr.304/HOL (2))

Holborn Viaduct was built across the Fleet Valley to improve the east-west flow of traffic to and from the City, and it was one of the most important road improvements to be made in London during the nineteenth century. Dixon photographed the progress of the work in a series of single-print images; he also created this panoramic view of the works to the west of Farringdon Road by joining together prints from three separate negatives.

56

1870 – 1899

S ANFORD worked from an address in Goldhawk Road, Shepherds Bush. He is not listed as a photographer in the trade directories and so was presumably either an amateur or photographed as an adjunct to some other trade.

JOHN SANFORD (ACTIVE 1870s)

'The Oxford Arms', Warwick Lane, c. 1870

Albumen print. Guildhall Library, Corporation of London (Norman Collection Vol 4)

'The Oxford Arms' was an old coaching inn, rebuilt in the late seventeenth century, which stood behind the Old Bailey. This photograph looks as though it must have been taken after 1868 when the rooms were let out to tenants, but probably it pre-dates the better-known views made for the Society for Photographing Relics of Old London by Alfred and John Bool in 1875. The building was demolished in 1877 or 1878.

HEDDERLY was a signwriter and painter who took up photography in the late 1860s. He spent his entire life in Chelsea and took quite a few photographs of the area in the early 1870s, especially the riverfront and Cheyne Walk.

JAMES HEDDERLY (c. 1815 – 1885)

Chelsea Riverfront from (old) Battersea Bridge, c. 1870

Albumen print. Guildhall Library, Corporation of London (Norman Collection Vol 2)

Hedderly lived in Duke Street, Chelsea, the back of which can be seen in this view. It was demolished to make way for Chelsea Embankment. The paddle-steamer is the 'Citizen' which probably plied between Chelsea and the City.

ANONYMOUS

**Octavious H. Smith's Thames Bank Distillery,
Grosvenor Road, SW1, c. 1870**

Albumen print. Guildhall Library, Corporation of London (B.W2/GRO)

Brewing was one of the largest manufacturing industries in London in the nineteenth century, so it is not surprising that it was one of the more frequently photographed. Few pictures were taken *inside* a brewery, or any other kind of factory, however, because the light levels were too low.

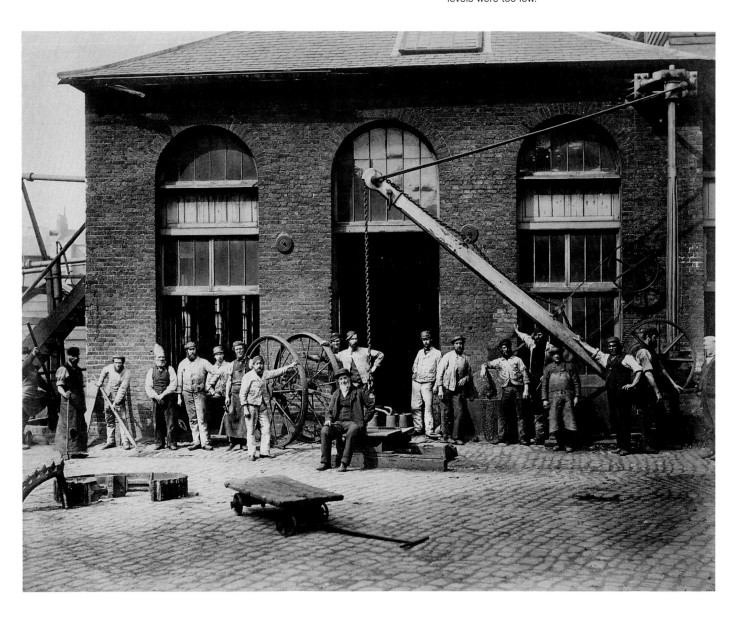

T HE Bool brothers were portrait painters who took up photography in the early 1870s. They opened at least one portrait studio in London, but are best known for their architectural work for the Society for Photographing Relics of Old London. The Society was started by a group of men who, in 1875, combined to commission a photographic record of the historic 'Oxford Arms' tavern in Warwick Lane *(see page 60)* which was threatened with demolition. The commission was given to the Bools who subsequently photographed other endangered buildings before their association with the Society came to an end in 1878.

ALFRED AND JOHN BOOL
(ACTIVE 1870s – 1880s)

Combe & Co.'s Brewery, Castle Street, St Giles, WC2, c. 1875
Carbon print. Museum of London (IN14842)

The Poor's Churchyard, St. Bartholomew's, Smithfield, 1877

Carbon print. Museum of London (IN1711)

This photograph was commissioned by the The Society for Photographing Relics of Old London. This group of houses was regarded by the Society as a picturesque survivor of old London, but to others it was a slum fit only for demolition.

MORGAN & Laing, a firm of commercial photographers based in Greenwich, was commissioned in 1875 to record the construction of Canada Dock, part of the Surrey Commercial Docks group. Two views of the completed dock are reproduced here to show the effect of the use of a cloud negative. This was printed in combination with the main negative to provide detail in the sky which would otherwise be blank owing to the over-sensitivity of the photographic plate to blue light. The same cloud negative has been used in both pictures, but it has been printed more strongly in one than in the other.

MORGAN & LAING

General View of Canada Dock, Surrey Commercial Docks, c. 1876

Albumen print. Museum of London/Port of London Authority Collection

General View of Canada Dock, Surrey Commercial Docks, c. 1876
Albumen print. Museum of London/Port of London Authority Collection

THOMSON travelled and photographed in the Far East for several years before he opened a studio in London in 1875. Two years later he collaborated with the left-wing journalist, Adolphe Smith, on a study of some of the poorer inhabitants of the capital, which was published as a part-work in 1877–1878 under the title, *Street Life In London*. In terms of the history of photography, *Street Life in London* is important because it was the first published collection of social documentary photographs anywhere. What is less clear, however, is its value as a serious work of social investigation. Opinion at the time was divided about its merit either as art or as propaganda, and there may well have been some disagreement between Thomson, the artist-photographer, and Smith, the radical socialist writer, about the content of the photographs. Following its issue as a part-work, *Street Life in London* was sold as a bound volume and then as a shortened version called *Street Incidents*. It is debatable whether this was due to the work's popularity or to the efforts of the publishers to get rid of unsold stock.

JOHN THOMSON (1837–1921)

The 'Crawlers', c. 1877

Woodburytype. Museum of London (IN648)

Of this photograph Smith wrote: *'Huddled together on the workhouse steps in Short's Gardens, those wrecks of humanity, the Crawlers of St. Giles's, may be seen both day and night seeking mutual warmth and mutual consolation in their extreme misery.'* The woman in the photograph was minding the child of a friend who had found a job in a coffee shop.

Recruiting Sergeants, Westminster, c. 1877

Woodburytype. Museum of London (IN621)

One of the army's principal recruiting centres in London was the street outside the 'Mitre and Dove' public house near Westminster Abbey. In his essay accompanying the photograph, Smith recorded that 3605 approved recruits were enlisted from the London district in 1875.

Hookey Alf, c. 1877

Woodburytype. Museum of London (IN647)

The title of the photograph refers to the man on the right who had lost his hand in an industrial accident. However, he is entirely up-staged by the little girl in the centre of the picture, with reference to whom Smith wrote: *'There is no sight to be seen in the streets of London more pathetic than this oft-repeated story – the little child leading home a drunken parent.'*

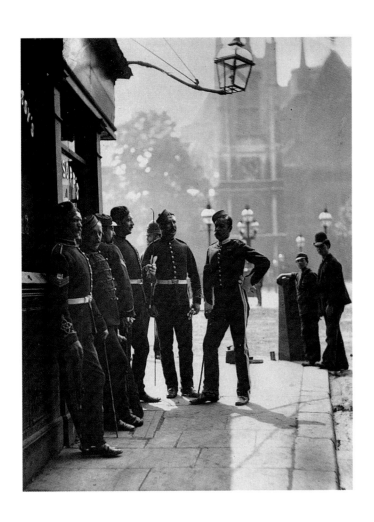

Workers on the Silent Highway, c. 1877

Woodburytype. Museum of London (IN641)

By the 1870s, as the result of major road improvements, the Thames had ceased to be London's main thoroughfare. Consequently the status of river workers such as the lightermen and bargemen had declined and their standard of living had fallen.

Covent Garden Labourers, c. 1877

Woodburytype. Museum of London (IN636)

Known as 'odd-men', quite a few of whom were of Irish descent and lived locally in the Seven Dials district, these casual labourers were employed by the market traders to deliver produce to their customers.

HENRY DIXON (1820–1893)
for biographical notes see page 56

St. Mary Overy's Dock, Southwark, 1881
Carbon print. Museum of London (IN1750)

Shambles in Aldgate, 1883

Carbon print. Museum of London (IN1770)

These old houses in Aldgate were demolished in 1880 to make way for the Metropolitan Railway's line from Aldgate to Tower Hill.

Shop in Macclesfield Street, Soho, 1883

Carbon print. Museum of London (IN1777)

Built in 1690, this was reputed to be the oldest surviving shop in London at the time of the photograph. It was demolished in 1885.

BEDFORD LEMERE (1839–1911)

T HE son of a draper and grocer, Lemere was a commercial traveller in the mid-1860s, but by 1870 he had established a reputation as an architectural photographer. He founded a company in the Strand and was joined by his son, Henry, in the early 1880s. In 1887, the company described itself as having the largest collection of architectural photographs in England, and it flourished under Henry Bedford Lemere's control until the Second World War.

Island Lead Mills, Limehouse, 1885

Albumen print. Royal Commission on Historic Monuments (5594)

This view was taken from a building on the Limehouse Cut looking north-west towards the Regent's Canal Dock, in which the masts of several tall ships are visible. The scene in the yard of the leadworks was clearly set up to show the unloading of barrels of what is, presumably, white lead. Lemere recorded several other industrial sites like this in London.

FOUNDED in 1854, the London Stereoscopic Company achieved great success as a mass-producer of stereoscopic views of famous buildings and places of interest in England and abroad. Following the decline in popularity of stereoscopic photographs in the late 1860s, the firm began to concentrate on taking and marketing conventional photographic views, including many of London's better-known streets. The company's founder, George Swan Nottage, became wealthy enough to be elected Lord Mayor of London in 1884, a year before he died.

ANONYMOUS FOR THE LONDON STEREOSCOPIC CO.

Regent's Quadrant, c. 1886

Albumen print. Museum of London (IN4090)

F RANCIS Godolphin Osbourne Stuart published a large number of views of London streets and architecture during the latter part of the nineteenth century. He worked from an address in St. Paul's Churchyard.

FRANCIS G. O. STUART (ACTIVE 1880s)

Trafalgar Square, c. 1885

Albumen print. Museum of London (IN4651)

Trafalgar Square was, and continues to be, one of the most photographed places in London. This is a particularly good late nineteenth-century view of it.

TRAFALGAR SQUARE 2338 F.C.O.S

O F the several nineteenth-century British photographic firms which specialised in topographical views, the company established in Aberdeen by George Washington Wilson was particularly noteworthy for the quality of its work. G. W. Wilson himself had photographed in London in the 1870s and from the mid-1880s his son, Charles, added to the company's stock of London negatives by taking a new set of photographs which included a series of candid street views taken from the back of a covered wagon.

CHARLES A. WILSON (1866 – ?)

Piccadilly Circus, c. 1890

Albumen print (gold toned). Museum of London (IN4633)

This view conveys brilliantly a sense of the importance of London at the end of the nineteenth century as the world's premier capital. Unlike most albumen prints which have faded to some extent over the years, those of the G. W. Wilson company have remained in superb condition, a testimony to the excellent craftsmanship of Wilson's printers. The rich purple colour was achieved by toning the print with gold.

Farringdon Street, Looking Towards Holborn Viaduct, c. 1890

Albumen print (gold toned). Museum of London (IN4111)

We used to hire a covered van from Pickford's, and stand with our 10" x 12" camera under the awning, fairly well out of sight of the passers-by, and then with the lens ready focused and capped and a dark slide inserted ready to draw, used to direct the driver to stop near the curb opposite some specified building, while we would watch our chance to make an instantaneous exposure.

Letter from Charles Wilson to Gernsheim (Gernsheim, 1955, p324)

The Great Wheel, Earl's Court Exhibition, c. 1890

Albumen print (gold toned). Museum of London (IN491)

An entertainment ground was opened at Earl's Court in 1887, and the Great Wheel was one of its permanent attractions.

Thames at Richmond, c. 1890

Albumen print (gold toned). Museum of London (IN4968)

PICCADILLY CIRCUS AND COVENTRY STREET, LONDON. 4050. G.W.W.

GREAT WHEEL AT EARLS COURT EXHIBITION.   9703.   G.W.W.

RICHMOND   BTT.   G.W.W.

C EMBRANO was described in *The Photographic Journal's* obituary of him as *'...one of the old school of pictorial photographers who chose pleasing and picturesque subjects'*. He was, it went on, particulary skilled at handling back-lit landscape views and was a regular exhibitor at the Royal Photographic Society, to which he was elected in 1890.

F. P. CEMBRANO [d.1912]

Pleasure Boats on the Thames, c. 1891

Unknown print. Royal Photographic Society (3281)

This photograph conveys a feeling of peace and tranquility which is in marked contrast to views taken by others further down-river towards the Pool of London and the docks.

ARTIN was a woodcut engraver by profession and a keen amateur photographer. In the early 1890s he obtained a 'Facile' detective magazine camera, disguised as a parcel, which could take several pictures before having to be reloaded. He made some improvements to the camera and roamed the streets of London with it to become one of the first to take candid snapshots of people in close-up. Martin's approach to photographing people, which required him to remain unnoticed in order not to influence the behaviour of his subjects, became *de riguer* for many reportage and documentary photographers in the twentieth century.

In 1899, with the demand for woodcut illustrations in serious decline, Martin took up photography professionally and became a partner in the firm of Dorrett and Martin. In 1939 he published a book of his photographs, called *Victorian Snapshots*, with an introduction by Charles Gibbs-Smith, then curator of the photography collection at the Victoria & Albert Museum, who wrote under the pseudonym of Charles Harvard. It is possible that the prints reproduced here are the ones originally made for that book.

PAUL MARTIN (1864–1944)

Street Urchins, Lambeth, 1893

Silver print, c. 1937. Victoria & Albert Museum (2889-1937)

> *I called them human squirrels, for when they caught sight of the school inspector, they were over a six-foot paling in a flash, and made off to 'Lambeth Walk'.*
>
> (Martin, 1939, page 14)

Dancing to the Organ, Lambeth, 1893

Silver print, c. 1937. Victoria & Albert Museum (2877-1937)

> The children are dancing to the *Pas de Quatre*, which was a famous Gaiety piece.

Blind Beggar, Caledonian Cattle Market, 1893–1894

Silver print, c. 1937. Victoria & Albert Museum (2912-1937)

A. J. RANSOME (ACTIVE 1890s)

Ransome was an early pictorial photographer about whom little is known.

The Frozen River, 1895

Platinum print. Royal Photographic Society (5042)

The Thames used to freeze over quite regularly, and in earlier centuries Londoners held 'Frost Fairs' on the ice. It froze over for the last time in the winter of 1895 when this photograph was taken.

Snow on the Embankment, 1896

Carbon print. Victoria & Albert Museum (1686-1980)

Enlarged carbon prints of Martin's night pictures, as here, were made by the Autotype Company. Using his 'Facile' hand camera mounted on a tripod, Martin successfully completed a series of night views of London in the 1890s which won him the Royal Medal at the Royal Photographic Society. The exposure time could be as much as half an hour, and Martin often attracted the attention of passing policemen. In 1939 he recalled that:

When I was making my first exposure on the Embankment in the pouring rain a bulky City policeman all complete with beard approached me and said, 'What are you supposed to be doing?' 'Taking a photograph,' I answered. 'What!' he exclaimed. 'At this time of night and in this rain?' 'Yes,' I replied. 'That's why I am taking it.' He said nothing more but stood by with his arms folded under his huge cape and just slightly nodding his head, as much as to say, 'Poor fellow! No doubt queer in the head!'

(Martin, 1939, page 25)

Magazine Seller, Ludgate Circus, 1893

Silver print, c. 1937. Victoria & Albert Museum (2900-1937)

The Old Empire Theatre, Leicester Square, 1895

Silver print, c. 1937. Victoria & Albert Museum (2880-1937)

UNDERWOOD and Underwood was a large photographic firm which specialised in the sale of stereoscopic views and news photographs. It was founded in Baltimore in 1886 by two brothers, Elmer and Bert Underwood, and had offices in New York, Chicago, Toronto, London and Paris. By 1901 the company was producing 25,000 photographs a day, a clear indication that an international mass market for photography had arrived.

ANONYMOUS FOR UNDERWOOD AND UNDERWOOD

Queen Victoria Driving Down Kensington Terrace, 28 June 1897

Albumen prints (stereo pair). Museum of London (IN14855)

The celebrations surrounding Queen Victoria's Diamond Jubilee in 1897 were an expression of London's status as *the* world city. The event coincided with a revival of interest in stereoscopic photography and this stereocard was distributed internationally by Underwood and Underwood.

(57) Queen Victoria Driving down Kensington Terrace, London, England, June 28th, 1897.
Copyright 1897 by Underwood & Underwood.

1900 – 1918

G ALT, a Scot, came to London in 1890 to work as a missionary for the London City Mission. In the early 1900s he took a series of photographs, mainly of the East End, which he made into lantern slides to illustrate lectures publicising the work of the Mission. Through the powerful combination of these graphic images and his skills as an orator, Galt sought to show that though there was great poverty in the East End, the people were not sub-human, as was popularly imagined by the middle-classes, but ordinary folk trying to do their best under difficult circumstances.

REV. JOHN GALT (1863–1942)

Backyards, Spitalfields, c. 1900

Modern silver print. Museum of London (IN488)

    The wooden structure in the centre of the photograph is a pigeon loft.

Making Shovels Out of Scrap Metal – a Home Industry, Bethnal Green, c. 1900

Modern silver print. Museum of London (IN434)

Railway Track Maintenance Gang, Outside St. Pancras Station, c. 1900

Modern silver print. Museum of London (IN483)

Cat's Meat Man in an East End Street, c. 1902

Modern silver print. Museum of London (IN432)

The decoration on the house celebrated the coronation of Edward VII in 1902.

DAVISON was a leading amateur photographer and also a founder member of the influential 'Linked Ring Brotherhood' of pictorialist photographers. He was also Managing Director of the Kodak Company Limited in London, and on a number of occasions he both tried out new Kodak cameras himself and lent them to some of his photographer friends, such as Paul Martin, to test. One of the new Kodak cameras Davison tried out himself was a swing-lens panoramic camera which he took onto the London streets.

GEORGE DAVISON (1856 – 1930)

Panorama of Traffic at a Busy Road Intersection, c. 1900

Platinum print. National Museum of Photography, Film & Television

Davison's street photographs taken to test new cameras, like the one shown here, are very different from his more controlled impressionistic studies, but the very randomness of the elements in the view is part of its attraction. The camera's lens swung through an angle of about 120 degrees.

I N the early years of the twentieth century, several local authorities began to engage photographers to record their new or expanded services. It is not known who took these beautifully composed photographs for the City of Westminster Council in 1903, but they are from a series of highly accomplished pictures showing council employees at work in the borough.

ANONYMOUS FOR THE CITY OF WESTMINSTER COUNCIL DEPARTMENT OF PUBLIC WORKS

Collecting Street Sweepings, 1903
Silver print. Museum of London (IN6655)

Repairing a Rock Asphalt Roadway, 1903
Silver print. Museum of London (IN6658)

MANY thousands of record photographs, many of them anonymous, have been taken in London's docks, both for individual dock companies and, after 1909, for the Port of London Authority.

ANONYMOUS FOR THE SURREY COMMERCIAL DOCKS ENGINEER'S DEPARTMENT

Warehousemen Loading Cheese onto a Special Loader, Canadian Produce Warehouse West, 1906

Silver print. Museum of London/Port of London Authority Collection

This is an early interior view, taken to publicise a new piece of commodity handling equipment, and the men have been carefully posed so that they would remain still during the exposure.

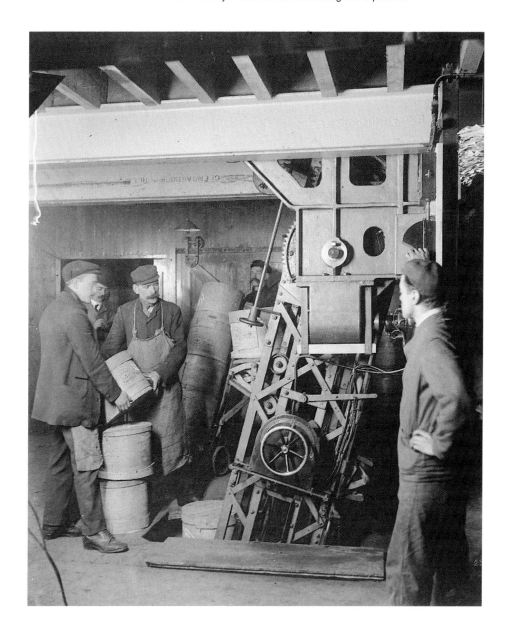

ITTLE is known about Avery other than that he special-ised in large-format record and progress photography and worked for clients such as the London County Council (LCC) and the Port of London Authority (PLA) between the early 1900s and the mid-1920s. His photographs exhibit a strong sense of pictorial composition unusual in this kind of photography, and he obviously took a great deal of trouble over his choice of viewpoint, which was often from an elevated position. The tonal gradation and amount of detail in his 12" x 10" contact prints could not have been achieved with a smaller negative format.

JOHN H. AVERY (ACTIVE 1900s – 1920s)

Drill With Barbells, Hugh Myddleton School, 1907

Silver print. Greater London Photograph Library

In 1904 the School Board for London was abolished and the LCC became the new education authority. This photograph is one of many excellent records of school buildings and educational activities which are believed to have been taken for the LCC by Avery. The photograph shows the girls practising 'callisthenics', which was an advanced training programme designed specifically to promote the physical development of girls.

Catherine Court, Trinity Square, 1913

Silver print. Museum of London/ Port of London Authority Collection

This beautifully composed and detailed photograph exemplifies Avery's concern for the descriptive quality of his pictures. It is one of several views commissioned by the Port of London Authority to record the area which was to be demolished to make way for its new headquarters in Trinity Square, opened by Lloyd George in 1922.

Panorama of the Site for County Hall, 1909

Silver prints (two), Greater London Photograph Library

This panoramic 'joiner' was commissioned by the LCC to record the site preparations for County Hall, built on the south bank of the Thames opposite the Houses of Parliament. The LCC moved into its new headquarters in 1922.

Excavating Machine, Royal Albert Dock Extension South, 11 September 1913

Silver print. Museum of London / Port of London Authority Collection

Avery's work for the Port of London Authority included much progress photography of dock construction. The London dock system covered many acres of land, and millions of tons of earth had to be moved with mechanical tools which appear primitive by the standards of the late twentieth century. In its time, however this steam-powered excavating machine was a piece of advanced engineering equipment. *See also pages 110–11.*

N American photographer of independent means, Coburn spent some time in London before settling there permanently in 1912. He learnt the photogravure process at the London County Council School of Photo-Engraving between 1906 and 1909 and acquired his own printing presses to make photogravure illustrations for his books. Coburn was a leading member of the international pictorialist movement, which had considerable influence over the status of photography as an artform during the first quarter of the twentieth century, and like many other pictorialists he was influenced by the work of the impressionist painters. A selection of Coburn's London views, printed by him in photogravure, were published under the title, *London*, in 1909. The images shown here are taken from this book.

ALVIN LANGDON COBURN (1882–1966)

Ludgate Hill, c. 1909

Photogravure. Museum of London (IN16000)

The atmospheric effects of smoke and steam were a feature of many pictorialist studies of urban scenes. This view, which Coburn took from the top-floor window of an office building in Ludgate Circus, was considerably altered in the early 1990s when the railway bridge in the foreground was removed and the line placed underground.

Hyde Park Corner, c. 1909

Photogravure. Museum of London

Wapping, c. 1909

Photogravure. Museum of London

Coburn was one of those photographers who found the working river romantic. There is a very strong resemblance between this photograph and a picture of the same part of the river painted in the 1860s by Whistler.

St. Paul's from the River, c. 1909

Photogravure. Museum of London

Regent's Canal, Camden Lock, c. 1909

Photogravure. Museum of London

Like many other pictorialists Coburn was fascinated with the visual effects of light on water.

C AMPBELL-GRAY was a commercial and portrait photographer who worked from a studio first in Cheapside and then, from 1911, in Edgware Road. His clients included the Church Army and the Port of London Authority.

CAMPBELL-GRAY (ACTIVE 1900s – 1910s)

Billingsgate Pier, 1907

Silver print. Museum of London (IN14853)

The pier was built in the late nineteenth century and accommodated a variety of vessels, including North Sea fishing-smacks, Dutch *schuyts*, Thames lighters and steam-tugs. Fresh fish were discharged straight from the boats into the fish market's cold store.

A Glass Lens Manufacturing Workshop, c. 1910

Silver print. Museum of London (IN3288)

The location of this workshop is not recorded, but it may well have been in Clerkenwell where there was a concentration of lens makers and other optical instrument manufacturers. Many London districts were traditionally associated with a particular type of product, such industries often being organised around small-scale workshops similar to the one shown here.

B ROOM was a professional topographical and press photographer and a supporter of the suffragette cause. She combined both activities by undertaking a project to record suffragette events in London and to make portraits of some of the leaders of the movement. These pictures are undoubtedly her best work and many were made into popular postcards.

CHRISTINA BROOM (1863–1939)

Miss Christabel Pankhurst at a Suffragette Fair, May 1909

Modern silver print. Museum of London (IN1334)

Christabel Pankhurst was a co-founder and leader of the Women's Social and Political Union. The photograph was taken at the Women's Exhibition at the Princes' Skating Rink in Knightsbridge in May 1909.

Suffragette Demonstration, May 1909

Modern silver print. Museum of London (IN1279)

The purpose of this procession through the West End of London was to advertise the 'Women's Exhibition and Sale of Works in the Colours' (ie the Suffragette colours of purple, white and green) which was to be held at the Princes' Skating Rink in Knightsbridge, 13–26 May 1909.

W HIFFIN was a portrait photographer with a strong interest in recording everyday life in Poplar in London's East End, where he lived and worked. He inherited his photographic business from his father shortly before the First World War and ran it until he retired in the 1950s. He undertook a wide range of commissions in addition to portraits and also photographed for himself. His interest in the history of London led him to photograph many old buildings and monuments, and some of his images were used to illustrate two books about London, published in the 1920s.

WILLIAM WHIFFIN (1878–1957)

Children Following a Water Cart, c. 1910

Silver print. Tower Hamlets Local History Library (Wh.682)

The water cart was once a familiar sight on London's streets, and playing in the spray was a popular children's pastime. *See also pages 122–23 and 201.*

NICHOLLS was an early freelance press photographer who had already made a name for himself photographing the Boer War before returning to London around 1900. He is best known for his photographs of the 'London Season', but he also made a number of superbly detailed views of London streets. In 1917 he was appointed the first official photographer of the Home Front.

HORACE W. NICHOLLS [1867–1941]

Ludgate Circus, c. 1910
Silver print. Royal Photographic Society (5493)

Derby Day, Epsom, 1912 or 1914
Modern toned silver prints (two). John Benton-Harris

Nicholls spent several years before the First World War photographing Edwardian High Society as it displayed itself at various annual summer sporting events in and around London. The man pointing in the foreground is Lord Astor. *See also pages 113–15.*

SINCLAIR, whose business was the manufacture of photographic equipment, came to London at the end of the nineteenth century. He was a keen amateur photographer who advocated the use of the hand camera together with a highly pictorial approach to image-making. He was an enthusiastic worker in the pigment processes of oil and bromoil, and he regarded these as allowing greater freedom of expression than was possible with standard photographic printing materials.

JAMES SINCLAIR (d. 1940)

The Haymarket in Winter, c. 1913

Photogravure print. Royal Photographic Society (4597)

Pictorialist photography was heavily influenced by the idea that to qualify as a work of art a photographic print had to be worked over by hand to give it a painterly quality. What the picture lost in terms of photographic detail as a result was often more than made up for by the dramatic effect which was obtained. Sinclair, like many pictorialist photographers, was interested in the atmospheric effects of smoke and fog.

S MYTH was the daughter of a wealthy Liverpool business-man. She came to London in 1911 where she became closely involved with the women's suffrage campaigner, Sylvia Pankhurst. Together they set up the East London Federation of Suffragettes (ELFS) which had its first headquarters in an old baker's shop in Bow Road. Smyth provided the ELFS with much-needed financial support and played a leading role in publishing its illustrated newspaper, the *Woman's Dreadnought*, for which she took photographs. The ELFS organised various educational and welfare activities for women and children during the First World War, including a cost-price restaurant and a nursery for the children of mothers who worked in the Federation's toy factory. These were the principal subjects of Smyth's photographs for the *Dreadnought*.

NORAH SMYTH [ACTIVE 1914–1915]

An Alley in Bromley, 1914

Modern silver print. International Institute of Social History, Amsterdam (A32/669)

This photograph of children in an alley near the Federation's clinic in Bromley-by-Bow was published in the *Womens' Dreadnought* on 22 August 1914.

A Child on a Bed in a House in Bow, 1915

Silver print. International Institute for Social History, Amsterdam (A32/668)

The child probably belonged to one of the workers at the ELFS toy factory in Norman Road, East London. The photograph was presumably taken in the child's home.

THERE are not many photographs of bomb damage in London during the First World War, and the set of views made by Miles & Kay, a firm of legal and technical photographers based in Cheapside, is one of the largest collections. This photographic record was almost certainly made for official purposes, perhaps for use as evidence in dealing with insurance claims.

MILES & KAY [ACTIVE 1915]

Addle Street from Wood Street, City of London, 8 September 1915

Silver print. Guildhall Library, Corporation of London (First World War Collection)

Liverpool Street, City of London, 8 September 1915

Silver print. Guildhall Library, Corporation of London (First World War Collection)

JOHN H. AVERY (ACTIVE 1900s–1920s)

for biographical notes see page 92

Quayside Crane in the Royal Victoria Dock
Damaged in the Silvertown Explosion, 2 February 1917

Silver print. Museum of London/ Port of London Authority Collection

Damage Caused to Grain Silos in the Royal Victoria Dock by the Silvertown Explosion, 25 January 1917

Silver print. Museum of London/ Port of London Authority Collection

On 19 January 1917 there was a huge explosion at the munitions factory of Messrs Brunner Mond & Co. Ltd, situated in Crescent Wharf in Silvertown. This caused extensive damage over a wide area, including part of the Royal Victoria Dock. Avery, who frequently worked for the Port of London Authority, was commissioned to make a photographic record of the damage to the dock, and using a 12" x 10" plate camera in appalling weather conditions he produced a most remarkable set of pictures.

ORTIMER was both a photographer and a journalist and was editor of the *Amateur Photographer and Photographic News* magazine between 1908 and 1918. He was a founder member of the London Salon of Photography and a member of the 'Linked Ring Brotherhood'. The purpose of 'the Ring' was to promote the artistic status of pictorial photography.

FRANCIS JAMES MORTIMER (1874–1944)

Soldiers Leaving for the First World War, c. 1915

Bromoil print. Royal Photographic Society (7551)

During the First World War this was a familiar scene at London's mainline railway stations serving the South Coast as soldiers departed to or returned from the Front.

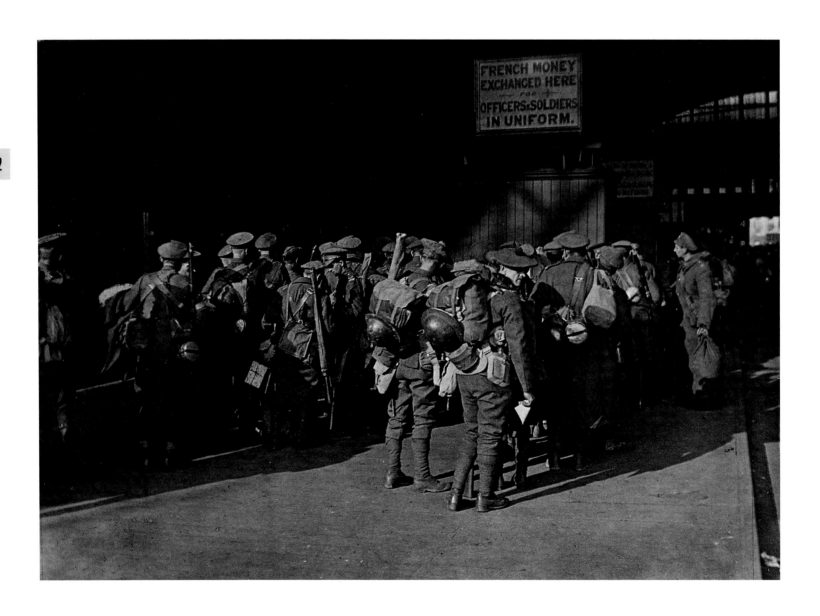

HORACE W. NICHOLLS (1867–1941)

for biographical notes see page 103

Wounded Soldier and Woman Flag-seller, 1918

Silver print. Royal Photographic Society (4719)

In 1918, Nicholls was commissioned by the newly-formed Imperial War Museum Committee to take a series of photographs of women doing jobs normally done by men, including heavy manual work and uniformed work. The photographs were intended to provide the museum with a visual archive for display purposes.

Women Spraying Tar, 1918

Silver print. Royal Photographic Society (7359)

Armistice Day Celebrations, Trafalgar Square, 1918

Silver print. Royal Photographic Society (23042)

1919 – 1939

THE founder of a firm of photographic postcard makers and a keen pictorialist, Judge invented a special camera for photographing at night and produced, in the 1920s, a set of views of London's nocturnal street life. He favoured the use of printing processes like the bromoil transfer process, invented by him, which allowed the image to be manipulated, so adding to the impressionistic effect.

FRED JUDGE (1872–1950)

So This is London, 1923
Bromoil transfer print. Royal Photographic Society (1607)

Held Up in Trafalgar Square, 1923
Bromoil transfer print. Royal Photographic Society (1611)

J ARCHÉ was one of the first generation of press photographers and his long career, which lasted from 1906 to 1959, included periods working for the *Daily Telegraph* (1906–1907), *Daily Sketch* (1912–1929), *(Weekly) Illustrated and Daily Herald* (1930–1953) and the *Daily Mail* (1953–1959). These and other newspapers ran regular photographic 'features', which usually comprised contrived and light-hearted pictures which were planned in advance. Jarché was adept at producing such images.

JAMES JARCHÉ (1890–1965)

Boys Caught Bathing in the Serpentine, 1924

Silver print. Royal Photographic Society (7145)

Jarché was working for the *Daily Sketch* when this photograph was taken. It is very similar to one taken by another press photographer, Reggie Speller, and it is highly likely that one or both pictures were set up for the camera.

J OB was a stockbroker who pursued artistic activities in his spare time and was particularly fond of photographing river scenes. An eminent pictorialist, he combined elements of naturalism and impressionism in his work and preferred photographing in the evening light when the shadows were long. He lived in Richmond from 1922 until his death.

CHARLES JOB (1853–1930)

Richmond Bridge, 1925

Carbon print. Royal Photographic Society (5314)

Below London Bridge, 1936

Carbon print. Royal Photographic Society (7171)

The contrasting nature of the subject matter of the two photographs here, leafy Richmond on the one hand and the industrialised Pool of London on the other, is somewhat blurred by Job's uniformly pictorial treatment.

WILLIAM WHIFFIN (1878–1957)

for biographical notes see page 102

Strikers Picketing a Van in Cotton Street, Poplar, During the General Strike, May 1926

Silver print. Tower Hamlets Local History Library (Wh.1104)

Whiffin's studio was near the junction of East India Dock Road and Cotton Street. During the General Strike of 1926 he found that the top floor window was a good vantage point for photographing activities in the street below. During the strike, pickets tried to prevent goods vehicles from entering or leaving the docks and their success eventually forced the authorities to use armed military convoys to keep the traffic flowing.

Manchester Road, Isle of Dogs, c. 1928

Silver print. Tower Hamlets Local History Library (Wh.233)

This view of the bow of a ship in dry dock overhanging the road is a variation of the photograph which is usually reproduced, and has the added interest of human activity on the street as well as up in the air. Whiffin took many photographs in the docklands area and was commissioned on occasion by the Port of London Authority.

DIXON-SCOTT was a topographical and landscape photographer working in the 1930s. Although the Port of London Authority (PLA) was then using its own staff photographers to record the docks and river, it occasionally commissioned outside photographers, including Dixon-Scott, to take additional pictures. Dixon-Scott's photographs have greater pictorial merit than most of those taken for the official record.

JOHN DIXON-SCOTT (ACTIVE 1930s)

The River at Gravesend, c. 1930

Silver print. Museum of London/Port of London Authority Collection

This photograph is one of the most pleasing studies of Thames shipping in the PLA Collection.

R EID was born in Sunderland and was a member of the Reid shipbuilding and brewing family. He was probably of independent means and had the time to develop his interests in photography and historical research. He studied the former with a professional, Benjamin Scott, in Carlisle in about 1900, and pursued his research as a member of the Newcastle Society of Antiquaries between 1904 and 1909. It is not known when he moved to London, but records show that in 1930–1931 he lived at 51 Grosvenor Road, SW, which later became part of Millbank. During these years he carried out a highly ambitious project to record, in photographs, an extended walk through the historic cities of Westminster and London. By the time of his death in 1933, he had taken over 700 photographs, organised geographically into a series of albums, and had compiled two manuscript books, entitled *The Route Ornate*, which served to annotate, in rhyme, the photographic journey. He composed his street views with a flair which is all the more remarkable given that he used a camera which had no viewfinder.

GEORGE DAVISON REID (1871–1933)

Southwark Corporation's Rubbish Depot, Greenmoor Wharf, Bankside, c. 1930

Silver print. Museum of London (IN9442)

Reid photographed several of the working wharves which lined the Thames on both banks . Here refuse – mainly dung swept up from the streets – was brought in by horse and cart and loaded onto barges by chutes and hydraulic crane.

125

Buckingham Palace Floodlit, c. 1930

Silver print. Museum of London (IN9071)

Reid made several night-time views as part of his extensive series on the cities of Westminster and London.

Trafalgar Square, c. 1930

Silver print. Museum of London (IN9125)

The Cobbled Causeway Under Southwark Bridge, c. 1930

Silver print. Museum of London (IN9462)

This delightful picture is rather atypical of Reid who normally chose not to pose the people in his photographs. The three well-dressed girls in the centre of the picture also appear in photographs taken at other locations, so it is possible that they are members of his family. The view is of the south bank looking east towards Cannon Street railway bridge.

Tower of London, c. 1930

Silver print. Museum of London (IN9528)

127

Bow Lane, c. 1930

Silver print. Museum of London (IN9394)

The 'Olde Watling' tavern, visible on the corner of the junction of Bow Lane and Watling Street, was one of the first buildings to be erected after the Great Fire of London in 1666. Behind it rises the tower of St. Mary Aldermary, designed by Sir Christopher Wren.

Piccadilly Circus, c. 1930

Silver print. Museum of London (IN9084)

CASPARIOUS was born in Berlin where his father was a textile merchant. He became interested in photography whilst training to be an actor in the late 1920s and took still photographs during the filming of various motion pictures. In 1930 he began to travel around the world taking photographs for German and Austrian newspapers, and after learning the techniques of colour photography in Vienna, he settled in London in 1938 where he opened the capital's first studio to specialise in commercial colour photography. After the Second World War he combined photography with documentary filmmaking.

HANS CASPARIOUS (1900 – c. 1980)

Pleasure Boats, 1930

Modern silver print. Museum of London (IN7844)

Few photographers seem to have documented leisure activities on the Thames in London and so this picture by Casparious is something of a rarity. It was taken on a visit to London in 1930.

ORN in Germany, Hoppé emigrated to Britain in 1900 and began working in a London bank. He became a professional portrait photographer in about 1907 and began to exhibit his work to wide acclaim. From the mid-1920s he concentrated on travel and landscape photography and produced a number of books before the Second World War, including several about London.

EMIL OTTO HOPPÉ (1878–1972)

A London Policeman, c. 1930

Silver print. Mansell Collection

Hoppé took a series of photographs of typical London characters to use as illustrations in his books. He reproduced this picture in both *London* (1932) and *The Image of London* (1935).

Bird's-eye View of the Northern Approach to London Bridge, Looking South, c. 1930

Silver print. Mansell Collection

London Bridge is a familiar photographic subject, taken here from an unusual vantage point. Almost as soon as it was opened in 1831, fears were expressed about the bridge's capacity to handle the ever-growing number of vehicles, and it soon became a symbol of London's worsening traffic problem. The bridge was a favourite location for photographers and other illustrators who wished to represent London's 'rush hour' congestion.

'Billy-cock' Hat Maker, c. 1930

Silver print. Mansell Collection

'Billy-cocks', or 'bobbin hats', were the distinctive headgear worn by porters at Billingsgate Fish Market. They were made of leather and tarred wood and are said to have been modelled on the helmets worn by bowmen at the battle of Agincourt.

HERE are over two hundred photographs in this series of snapshots of passers-by, all taken in the same location. The unknown photographer was clearly someone skilled in the the use of the recently-introduced (and expensive) 35mm camera. It is interesting to note that in nearly every case the photographer took the picture just as the subject became aware of the camera. Whatever the motives of the photographer in taking these pictures, this unique collection provides a fascinating glimpse of everyday life between the wars in one of London's prosperous outer suburbs.

ANONYMOUS

Shoppers in Sutton High Street, c. 1930

Silver prints (four). Museum of London

FOX Photos was founded in 1926 by Richard Fox, Ernest Beavor and Reginald Salmon. The company provided a service in press and industrial photography, but none of the photographers who worked for the agency were ever credited, so there names were largely unknown to the public. The Fox Photos library was acquired by the Hulton Deutsch collection in the 1980s.

ANONYMOUS FOR FOX PHOTOS

Unemployed Girls Queuing for Work in Farringdon Street, March 1931

Silver print. Museum of London (IN7860)

Despite the diverse economy of the capital, many Londoners suffered unemployment during the economic depression of the 1930s, though conditions were not as bad as in the other industrial cities elsewhere in Britain. This press photograph is particularly evocative of the period, the feeling aroused by the subject being reinforced by the dull, hazy light which was then characteristic of London's polluted atmosphere. The photographer's use of differential focus adds to the effect. *See also page 174.*

Children Playing Cricket in Alpha Road, Millwall, 1938

Silver print. Museum of London (IN4096)

SPENDER began photographing in London in 1934 whilst studying to be an architect. At the time he was influenced by the idea that many of the social problems in poor urban areas were due to sub-standard housing, and that by applying the right sort of architectural principles (ie those based on the ideas of people like Le Corbusier, Mies van der Rohe and Gropius), some of these problems could be solved. Spender made the acquaintance of a probation officer who gained him entry to homes in Stepney so that he could take photographs of the living conditions of the inhabitants. After finishing his architectural studies, Spender became a full-time photographer and set up a studio in the Strand. He began to work for the *Daily Mirror* and in 1937 he joined Tom Harrison's Mass Observation team on an unpaid part-time basis to photograph life on the streets of Bolton and Blackpool as part of an anthropologically motivated study of working-class people in the north of England. From 1938 until he enlisted in the army in 1941, he worked for *Picture Post* magazine. After the War he devoted his time to painting and textile design.

HUMPHREY SPENDER (b. 1910)

A Woman Leaving a Pub with a Gramophone, Whitechapel, c. 1938

Modern silver print. Museum of London (IN7286)

This is from a series of photographs of Whitechapel which Spender took for *Picture Post.*

Family Group at Home, Stepney, c. 1934

Modern silver print. Museum of London (IN7285)

Spender was an early user of one of the new 35mm miniature cameras, a Contax, which was fitted with a fast lens. With it he was able to take unposed photographs of people inside their homes in Stepney using only available light.

N the early 1930s Man worked as a photo-reporter for German illustrated magazines such as the *Münchner Illustrierte Presse* and the *Berliner Illustrierte Zeitung*. He came to England in 1934 and began to work for the newly established *Weekly Illustrated* magazine. This had been set up by Stefan Lorant, the former editor of the *Münchner Illustrierte Presse*, and was based on the continental model. Man left after a few months, however, and worked as a freelancer until 1938. He then teamed up with Lorant again on the new *Picture Post* magazine, of which the latter was the first editor. Man continued his association with *Picture Post* until 1950 and then left to concentrate on other work.

FELIX H. MAN (1893 – 1985)

A Pub in the Edgware Road, 1938

Silver print. Lieselott Man

Man photographed several magazine stories about London before the Second World War and this picture was taken on one of these assignments.

Piccadilly Circus, 1934

Silver print. Lieselott Man

Man contributed pictures to a photo-essay on London's nightlife which was published by *Weekly Illustrated* magazine in 1934. He used one of the new German-made miniature cameras – a Leica – whose speed made candid night shots like this possible.

An East End Street, 1936

Silver print. Lieselott Man

Like many other photo-reportage and documentary photographers in the 1930s, Man photographed in the East End. This part of London was known primarily for its poverty and was the subject of many photo-stories and documentary investigations. The street play of children is an ever-popular photographic subject.

MURCH, a banker by profession, was noted for his romantic approach to photography and for his picturesque lighting effects. He thought of pictorial photography as being about 'the poetry of light', and that philosophy is exemplified by the pictures shown here.

HORACE A. MURCH (1895 – 1969)

Busy Thames n.d.

Unknown print. Royal Photographic Society (6638)

The location of this dramatic photograph is not recorded, but the industrial nature of the scene suggests that it was probably taken somewhere down-river of the Pool of London.

Nightfall at Westminster n.d.

Unknown print. Royal Photographic Society (6641)

The photograph must have been taken from a point on the south bank close to County Hall, and the evening mist has contributed greatly to the overall pictorial effect.

B LAKE was a member of the prestigious group of pictorialist photographers known as the Linked Ring Brotherhood which was active during the early years of the twentieth century. He was a regular contributor under the pseudonym 'Cockney'.

A. H. BLAKE [ACTIVE c. 1900 – 1915]

An Evening Train Leaving Cannon Street, n.d.

Carbon print. Royal Photographic Society (538)

The picture here is a fine example of impressionism in photography, the Thames being a favourite subject with pictorialist photographers.

WOLFGANG SUSCHITZKY (b.?)

ORN in Austria, Suschitzky came to London in about 1933 and in 1937 began to work for the Strand Film Company as a documentary film cameraman. He went on to enjoy a distinguished career in film and television, and combined this work with freelance photography for a variety of clients. Drawn by its large number of bookshops (his father owned a bookshop in Vienna), he embarked upon a personal photographic portait of Charing Cross Road in the mid-1930s. A selection of the work was published in 1988 under the title, *Charing Cross Road in the Thirties*. In his introduction to the book, the historian, Raphael Samuel, wrote: *'It is one of the merits of Wolf Suschitzky's photographs that they bring out, and indeed celebrate, Charing Cross Road's promiscuous mix of activities.'* (Suschitzky, 1988).

Two Men in a Café, Charing Cross Road, c. 1935

Modern silver print. Museum of London (IN15420)

Milk Cart, Charing Cross Road, c. 1935

Modern silver print. Museum of London (IN15411)

Victoria Bus Station, 1939

Modern silver print. Museum of London (IN15415)

In the days before mass car ownership, travel by road in London usually meant going by bus. Victoria Bus Station was the hub of a complex web of routes reaching out to all parts of the capital.

Fog in the Charing Cross Road, c. 1935

Modern silver print. Museum of London (IN15413)

This view looking south near Cambridge Circus was taken during one of London's legendary 'pea-soupers', the background all but obliterated by the swirling fog. The picture is very much part of a popular late twentieth-century image of what London used to be like, an image constantly reinforced by the film and television industry whose period London dramas invariably use synthetic fog as a neat way of avoiding the expense of creating authentic-looking backdrops.

MONCK was a candid street photographer who worked in London in the 1930s, concentrating on the poorer working-class inner suburbs. She photographed for personal rather than for professional reasons and belonged to the tradition of social observers which had earlier informed the work of the pioneering street photographer, Paul Martin *(see page 80)*. Many of her photographs were taken in Portland Town in North London during the demolition of the area, or in the Saffron Hill district of Clerkenwell, known as 'Little Italy' because of its large Italian population. Like others at the time, she also photographed in the East End, although she did not single out the area for particular attention.

MARGARET MONCK (1911–1991)

Goods Way, Near Kings Cross, c. 1935

Modern silver print. Museum of London (IN15204)

The area to the north of Kings Cross Station featured an extensive railway goods yard, the Regent's Canal and the ornate Victorian cast-iron gasholders which dominate the background in this picture. The bleakness of industrial London is well captured here.

Woman with a Camera, Portland Town, c. 1935

Silver print. Museum of London (IN14983)

Italian Seller of Windmills Saffron Hill, c. 1935

Modern silver print. Museum of London (IN15129)

ORN in Russia, Arapoff was forced to leave after the 1917 Revolution, and following a period spent mostly in Paris and in Germany, he settled in England in 1933. Having developed an interest in photography he established a portrait studio in Oxford, where his success led him to become the official photographer to the Anton Dolin Ballet. He also freelanced for various magazines which published extended photo-stories, and carried out personal documentary projects, several of which were concerned with aspects of life in London. His work was regularly exhibited during the 1930s and was often featured in the photographic press of the time. He used a miniature rollfilm camera, a 4cm x 4cm Rolleiflex, and was sponsored by the company which imported the camera into Britain in return for the use of his name in its advertising. Following some experience as a stills cameraman in the late 1930s, Arapoff was taken on as a film cameraman by the Strand Film Company in 1941, and from then on he pursued his career in the documentary film industry.

CYRIL ARAPOFF (1898–1976)

Carpet Stall, Caledonian Market, 1935

Silver print. Museum of London (IN14290)

Before the Second World War, the Caledonian Market in Islington was one of London's biggest weekend street markets. Arapoff photographed it extensively in the mid-1930s, and other documentary photographers (notably Bill Brandt and Edith Tudor-Hart) worked there too.

East End Girl, c. 1935

Silver print. Museum of London (IN14624)

Like many other documentary photographers and photo-reporters in the 1930s, Arapoff was drawn to London's East End because of its reputation for having the capital's worst social problems. Arapoff's approach was sympathetic rather than radical, and he concentrated particularly on photographing children in the street.

Mr Mix with his Children, Hanbury Buildings, Poplar, 1939

Silver print. Museum of London (IN14508)

In 1939 Arapoff teamed up with a writer, Jack Barker, and together they obtained a commission from *Picture Post* to produce a photo-story on living conditions in a run-down tenement block in Poplar, East London. The photograph shows one of the tenants and his children just before the start of a rent strike. *Picture Post* did not run the story, but the tenants did succeed in winning a rent reduction from the landlord. However, within a few months the building had been destroyed by a German bomb.

St. Martin's Church from the National Gallery, c. 1935

Silver print. Museum of London (IN14349)

Whilst in Germany, Arapoff had come into contact with new developments in photography there, which included the use of fast-acting miniature rollfim cameras and an emphasis on unusual viewpoints and angles as pictorial devices. The influence of this *Neue Sachlichkeit,* or 'New Objectivity', is evident here.

Wapping, c. 1935

Silver print. Museum of London (IN14289)

Thames at Kew Bridge, c.1935

Silver print. Museum of London (IN14614)

Arapoff had a particular interest in waterways and he photographed extensively both the Thames and the Regent's Canal in the mid-1930s. His best photographs of the river show it as an industrial enterprise.

ERMAN by birth, Brandt had English roots. He lived in Paris from 1929–1930, and then settled in London where as a freelance photographer, he became fascinated by the documentary possibilities of the city. He was particularly concerned, during the 1930s, with the contrast between the rich and poor in English society. His own wealthy family connections in London provided access to one end of the social spectrum, and the other was available for all to see in London's streets, cafés and pubs. Brandt was adept at the 'fly-on-the-wall' approach, where the subjects of his photographs appear to be oblivious to the presence of either himself or his camera. However, not everything is as it seems in his photographs, and he often staged his pictures, sometimes using his family or friends as models. Many of Brandt's images were commissioned by illustrated magazines, such as *Weekly Illustrated*, *Picture Post* and *Lilliput*. During the War he worked for the government and in 1940 he made a documentary record of some of London's underground shelters. The post-War period saw his career change direction and he began to concentrate on portraits, landscapes and nudes. *See also page 167, 168 and 169.*

BILL BRANDT (1904–1983)

Workman's Café, c. 1936

Silver print. Museum of London (IN2238)

This photograph was used by Brandt in his first book, *The English at Home* (1936), where it appeared opposite a photograph taken inside a gentleman's club in St James's. Such pairings were a feature of Brandt's documentary approach.

Parlourmaid and Underparlourmaid Ready to Serve Dinner, c. 1936

Modern silver print (probably from a copy negative). J-P Kernot

Access to the upper echelons of London society was relatively easy for Brandt because of his family connections. Many of his photographs showing life 'upstairs' were taken in his father's London house, which is where this picture was made. It is one of a series which Brandt took on assignment for a magazine on the theme of 'a day in the life of' a servant. In an interview with the author, Brandt explained that his reason for taking these photographs had been his realisation that the practice of employing large numbers of servants, like those shown here, was rapidly becoming a thing of the past.

A 'Bobby' on Point Duty, c. 1936

Silver print. J-P Kernot

Brandt's documentary photographs often go beyond a mere description of appearances. Here the London policeman, a familiar figure in 1930's street photographs, is not just a controller of traffic but has been transformed into a potent symbol of the power and authority of the state in Britsh society.

After the Theatre or By No Means The Last Days of an Old Taxi, Lower Regent Street, c. 1936

Modern silver print (probably from a copy negative). J-P Kernot

This photograph is a classic image of London's pre-War nightlife. Clearly staged for the camera (and flashgun), the man standing on the taxi's running board is Brandt's actor brother, Rolf, who features in several of Brandt's documentary-style photographs. The taxi driver was, apparently, a well-known character of the time.

ARTIER-BRESSON is widely regarded as the supreme master of the intuitive art of recognising and responding in an instant to the photographic possibilities of whatever situation he is in – capturing, as he put it, the 'decisive moment'. He trained as a painter in Paris and studied art and literature at Cambridge University. He became a freelance photographer and filmmaker in the 1930s. He was one of the founders of the Magnum Photos agency, set up in 1947, and chose to specialise in covering events in the East. However, he photographed in London on several occasions, both before and after the Second World War, where he documented important events such as George VI's Coronation (1937) and funeral (1952). He also photographed everyday scenes in London which are less well-known than some of his other work.

HENRI CARTIER-BRESSON (b.1908)

Coronation of George VI, 1937

Modern silver print. Magnum Photos

As a freelance photo-reporter working for the French communist magazine, *Ce Soir*, Cartier-Bresson documented the Coronation in a very different way from that expected of a press photographer. Instead of choosing a fixed location from which to record the Coronation procession as it passed, he ignored the event's official spectacle altogether, roamed around, and photographed the spectators, whose behaviour he found to be infinitely more interesting. *See also pages 205, 206.*

GRIGGS originally trained as an artist and musician and became involved in photography whilst serving with the RAF during the First World War. Later, he specialised in producing dramatised pictures of industrial subjects, and also earned commendation for his experiments in colour photography.

NOEL GRIGGS [1890 – 1942]

Battersea Power Station, c. 1937

Bromoil print. Royal Photographic Society (1811)

Battersea Power Station, designed by Sir Giles Scott, was one of a string of architecturally distinguished coal-fired power stations built along the banks of the Thames during the 1930s to provide electricity for London's rapidly increasing industrial and domestic requirements. When built in 1937 it had only two chimneys, but a later extension doubled this to four.

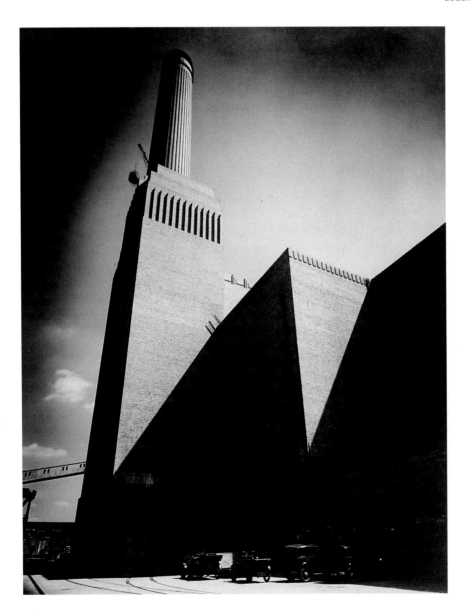

KERSTING began his career as an architectural and travel photographer in the 1930s. He served with the RAF Photographic Unit in the Middle East during the Second World War, and afterwards travelled in a number of different countries photographing for various books. He was particularly noted for this photography of Islamic architecture.

ANTHONY KERSTING (b. 1916)

The Embankment and Cleopatra's Needle from Hungerford Brigde, c. 1937
Silver print. Museum of London (IN4772)

1940 – 1945

MASON was a staff photographer with the *Daily Mail*. His name remained virtually unknown to the general public, yet he took what became perhaps the most famous photograph of London. To his colleagues Mason was known as a quiet and unobtrusive man who was nevertheless always keen to produce first-class results whatever the circumstances.

HERBERT MASON (1903 – 1964)

St Paul's Cathedral During the Blitz, 29 December 1940

Silver print. Museum of London

This photograph was taken from the roof of the *Daily Mail* building in Fleet Street after one of the worst nights of bombing experienced by the City of London, sometimes known as the 'Second Fire of London'. It appeared in the following day's paper above the headline, *War's Greatest Picture* and instantly entered the nation's conscious as *the* visual icon of the British wartime spirit of survival.

BILL BRANDT (1904 – 1983)

for biographical notes see page 156

East End Underground Station Shelter, 12 November 1940

Silver print. Museum of London (IN8719)

South East London Underground Station Shelter, 11 November 1940

Silver print. Museum of London (IN8704)

Commissioned by the Ministry of Information, Brandt took a series of about thirty-five photographs inside underground shelters over a two-week period in November 1940. His brief was to create an official record of the conditions there, and in that context it is interesting to note that some of the photographs show definite signs of having been set up. In the picture below, for example, it is most unlikely that anyone would in reality lie on the platform with their head so close to the passing trains. Throughout the series there is a strong sense of the surreal, something which Brandt went on to explore more fully after the War.

South East London Underground Station Shelter, 11 November 1940

Silver print. Museum of London (IN8727)

CROSS and Tibbs were City of London policemen and keen amateur photographers. Cross was appointed official photographer to the police department in 1939, and when the Blitz on London began in September 1940 he was instructed as part of his duties to record the damage caused to the City night after night by the German bombers. Tibbs was assigned to assist him in this task and early each morning following a night raid they went out with their cameras to photograph the devastation. Out of the ruins of the blitzed City, nearly a third of which was destroyed between September 1940 and May 1941, Cross and Tibbs created a unique and comprehensive visual record of London during one of the most momentous periods in its modern history, and in so doing they made some beautiful photographs.

ARTHUR CROSS AND FRED TIBBS
(ACTIVE 1940s)

Queen Street Place Looking South Towards Southwark Bridge, 11 May 1941
Silver print. Museum of London (IN7023)

Lower Thames Street, 29 December 1940
Silver print. Museum of London (IN6912)

City Temple, Holborn Viaduct, 17 April 1941

Silver print. Museum of London (IN6942)

Moorgate Station, 29 December 1940

Silver print. Museum of London (IN6845)

Corn Exchange, 42 Mark Lane, 17 April 1941

Silver print. Museum of London (IN6941)

ANONYMOUS FOR FOX PHOTOS

for notes see page 136

A Policeman Inspecting Bomb Damage, 1940 or 1941

Modern silver print. The Hulton Deutsch Collection

This picture conveys the pathos of the situation well, with the policeman not knowing what he is going to find buried in the rubble. At the same time the photographer carefully avoids actually showing that bombs kill and maim people. This restrained approach is in marked contrast to later war photography.

KEYSTONE Press was founded in 1920 by a Hungarian émigré, Bert Garai. He ran the press agency from premises in Red Lion Court, off Fleet Street, until 1964, when it was taken over by his son. In 1981 the company was sold by the Garai family and is now owned by Hulton Deutsch. *See also page 185.*

ANONYMOUS FOR KEYSTONE PRESS

Police Officers Attending to an Injured Man, 20 October 1940

Modern silver print. The Hulton Deutsch Collection

An uncredited press photograph with clear propaganda value. Some press photographers exploited to great effect a feature of their large-format folding plate cameras which was not available to users of miniature rollfilm cameras. This was the relatively narrow depth of field of the standard lens which caused the subject nearest the camera to be sharply focused whilst everything else was thrown distinctly out of focus, thus creating a more dramatic effect.

AFTER working for the BBC in London, Rodger became a freelance photojournalist in 1939 and was a war correspondent for the American *Life* magazine until 1945, when he joined the staff. As a 'stringer' for *Life* he could effectively shoot his own stories and he decided to concentrate on the effects of the German bombing on everyday life during the London Blitz of 1940. In 1947 he became a founder member of the Magnum photographic agency and subsequently specialised in photographing on the African continent.

GEORGE RODGER (1908 – 1995)

Blind Beggar, Hyde Park Corner, 1940
Modern silver print. Magnum Photos

Two Boys with a Steel Helmet, 1940
Modern silver print. Magnum Photos

ANONYMOUS FOR TOPICAL PRESS

Home on Leave from BEF, Soldier Says Goodbye to his Baby Son, 13 June 1940

Modern silver print. Museum of London (IN16423)

Evacuation of London School Children, Soldier Saying Goodbye to his Son, 13 June 1940

Modern silver print. Museum of London (IN16423-detail)

These appealing photographs typify the kind of propaganda images used by the press in wartime. They are, in fact, prints made from the same negative, but were given different captions to suit a particular story. Which caption is the true one? Possibly neither of them!

A FTER spending most of the 1930s working for photographic agencies, and for a short period for himself, Hardy joined the staff of *Picture Post* in 1940. He stayed with the magazine until it closed in 1957 and then, believing that a chapter in British photojournalism had come to an end, he worked in the field of advertising. *See also pages 190, 191, 192 and 193.*

BERT HARDY (1913 – 1995)

Children Running After the Parson, 23 November 1940

Modern silver print. The Hulton Deutsch Collection

The man in the photograph was the Rev. French, Rural Dean of Stepney, who was photographed by Hardy for a wartime *Picture Post* story called 'The East End Parson'. Hardy recalled that the scene was staged for the camera, but no doubt the picture accurately reflects the fondness the children had for this man who was providing valuable support for people whose homes had been destroyed by bombing.

Man with an Injured Leg, 18 January 1941

Modern silver print. The Hulton Deutsch Collection

Hardy took a series of photographs for use in a *Picture Post* story about rescue workers. This is one of them and, unsurprisingly, it was not used. Photographs like this are quite rare as photographers and editors knew very well that such pictures would not pass the censor and might even jeopardise the photographer's continuing entitlement to a permit.

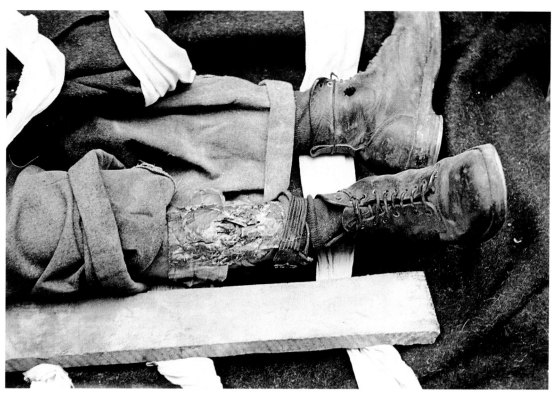

Firefighter, 11 January 1941

Modern silver print. The Hulton Deutsch Collection

Hardy climbed onto the roof of a building in order to get this picture of firemen tackling a warehouse blaze in the City. It was published by *Picture Post* on 1 February 1941 as part of a photo-feature called 'Fire-fighters'. It earned Hardy the distinction of being the first *Picture Post* staff photographer ever to be credited in the magazine.

OCCASIONALLY a name can be put to the author of an anonymous agency photograph if he or she is featured in a photographic book. Speller was a press photographer who began working just as the First World War started and continued a career as staff photographer with Fox Photos until he retired in the 1960s.

REGGIE SPELLER (1898–1981) FOR FOX PHOTOS

The Southern Railway Home Guard Receiving Tommy Gun Instruction, 11 March 1942

Modern silver print. The Hulton Deutsch Collection

ANONYMOUS

Bombed Houses, 1943

Dufaycolour. Royal Photographic Society

The date of this photograph indicates that the damage was caused by a V1, or 'flying bomb' as it was known. The collective image of the Second World War is conditioned by seeing photographs and film in black and white, and so it comes as a shock to see a scene like this photographed in colour. It looks so much like a still from a modern television reconstruction that it is difficult to believe that the photograph is genuine.

ANONYMOUS FOR KEYSTONE PRESS

for notes see page 175

VE Day Celebrations, Piccadilly Circus, 8 May 1945

Modern silver print. The Hulton Deutsch Collection

The typical large-format press camera of the period used either single or double film and plate holders which restricted the photographer to taking only one or two pictures at a time. Press photographers therefore had to learn how to anticipate the best moment to take their picture rather than rely on shooting a sequence of photographs for later editing. This skill is shown to good effect here.

1946 – 1969

HOPKINS began his career as a Fleet Street press photographer in the late 1930s and then served with the RAF Photographic Unit between 1939 and 1945. Following a period freelancing for newspapers and magazines, he worked as a photojournalist for *Picture Post* from 1949 until 1957, when the magazine closed.

THURSTON HOPKINS (b.1913)

Gypsy Horse Dealers, Elephant and Castle, 1948

Silver print. Museum of London (IN15925)

This photograph was taken whilst Hopkins was working as a freelance photojournalist. The Elephant and Castle had a reputation for being one of the poorest parts of the country, and the following year Bert Hardy was sent by *Picture Post* to do a story about it. *See page 191.*

North London Wedding Party, 1958

Silver print. Museum of London (IN15950)

Following the closure of *Picture Post*, Hopkins went back to freelance work, this time chiefly in advertising. The photograph here is one of a series he took for Shell BP called *Scenes from British Life and Leisure.*

BERT HARDY (1913–1995)

for biographical notes see page 180

Couple in a Room, Elephant and Castle, 1949

Silver print. The Hulton Deutsch Collection

After the Second World War, Bert Hardy and his *Picture Post* colleague, the left-wing journalist Bert Lloyd, worked together on a series of stories for the magazine about poverty in Britain. One of these concerned life in the Elephant and Castle in South London, an area close to where Hardy had grown up. They wandered around the streets looking for pictures and were introduced to the couple featured in this photograph.

Eddie, the Shoe-Black, Piccadilly, c. 1952

Silver print. The Hulton Deutsch Collection

Hardy took a series of street photographs in and around Piccadilly Circus to illustrate a *Picture Post* story published in 1952. He was free to photograph almost any aspect of daily life in the area, and he adopted a candid camera approach in order not to be observed by his subjects.

190

'You're Never Alone with a Strand', Albert Bridge, 1959

Silver print. The Hulton Deutsch Collection.

In 1959, two years after the demise of *Picture Post*, Hardy started working in advertising. He used a 35mm camera and a reportage approach, and photographed a successful campaign for Strand cigarettes. This involved spending a night on the streets of London with two models and a powerful torch. The result was this memorable picture which was probably the first 35mm photograph to be made into a 48-sheet poster.

BORN in London, Stone completed a series of views of the capital in the late 1940s to celebrate the fact that it had survived the War.

JOHN H. STONE (ACTIVE 1940s)

Pool of London, c. 1948

Silver print. Museum of London (IN15544)

This photograph was taken looking east from London Bridge. It shows vessels moored at Fresh Wharf in the foreground and, on the other side of the river, larger ships at Hays Wharf, which was one of the busiest wharves in the Upper Pool.

HENDERSON worked in various media, including photography, and was a pioneer of English Pop Art. He was a highly-respected artist who was one of the founders of the Independent Group at the Institute of Contemporary Art in the early 1950s. He freelanced for magazines and, later, taught photography at various art colleges.

NIGEL HENDERSON (1917–1985)

Group Outside a Pub in Hammersmith on Boat Race Day, c. 1952

Silver print. Museum of London (IN7526)

This photograph of well-to-do Boat Race supporters contrasts with the majority of Henderson's street photographs which were taken in the East End of London where he lived between 1945 and 1952.

A FREELANCE photographer, Grant worked extensively in London and often collaborated with his journalist wife, Rose, on stories for newspapers and magazines. As active supporters of social and political reform, they worked on many stories related to contemporary issues, such as the coverage of demonstrations and strikes. A great deal of their work was concerned with education, and it is for this that they are best known.

HENRY GRANT (b. 1907)

Street Entertainer, c. 1950

Silver print. Museum of London/Henry Grant Collection

Many of Grant's street photographs were taken on his way home from an assignment as a productive way of using up the film in his camera. The resulting pictures were then added to his growing library of stock photographs for possible use in the future.

Youths Looking in a Clothes Shop Window, c. 1950

Silver print. Museum of London/Henry Grant Collection (1301/5)

The theme of American influences on the development of British youth culture is one which was picked up by several photographers in the 1950s and 1960s (*see Liebling, page 221, and Spencer, page 224*). As social observers they were quick to realise that clothing and hair styles were becoming important indicators of cultural identity and social grouping amongst young people.

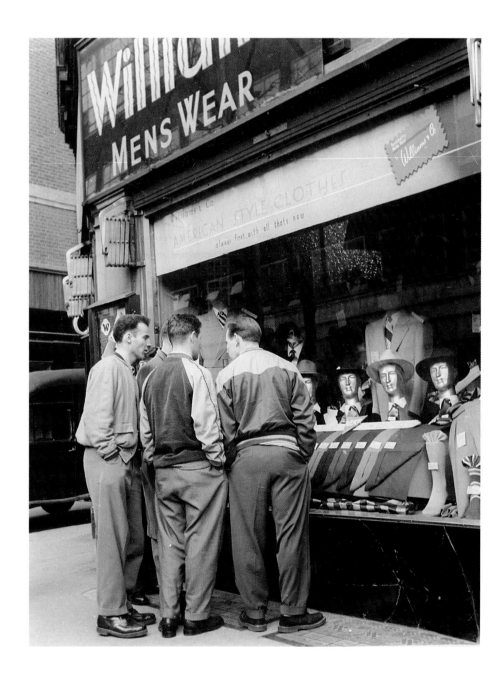

Striking Dock Workers, 1951

Silver print. Museum of London/Henry Grant Collection (1309/41)

The Dock Strike of 1951 was part of a campaign to abolish the 'call-on' system of casual labour in the docks. This was finally achieved in the 1960s, just a few years before London's docks began to be run down prior to closure in the 1970s.

Striking Dock Workers, 1951

Silver print. Museum of London/Henry Grant Collection (1309/24)

H ARKER was a professional architectural photographer from 1942 to 1960. She worked for the National Buildings Record during the War, then for various clients including several well-known architects. In 1959 she was appointed Head of the School of Photography at the Polytechnic of Central London, later the University of Westminster, and went on to pursue a distinguished career in education and as a photographic historian.

MARGARET HARKER (b. ?)

St. Paul's Cathedral from Cheapside, 1952

Silver print. Margaret Harker

This fine portait of St. Paul's shows the Cathedral as it was viewed from the north before the building of Paternoster Square in the 1960s, a development which was later widely criticised.

WILLIAM WHIFFIN (1878–1957)

for biographical notes see page 102

Hilary House, Teviot Street, Bromley, Under Construction, c. 1953

Silver print. Tower Hamlets Local History Library (Wh.1443)

The rebuilding of London's bomb-damaged East End meant that a large number of high-rise tower blocks were constructed. They were seen as the ideal solution to post-War housing problems, but the judgement of history has been somewhat different.

A LITHUANIAN Jew, Bidermanas went to Paris in 1930 where he became a portrait photographer. After the War, during which he was forced to hide from the German occupying forces, he turned to photojournalism and worked for *Paris Match* magazine. Following the success of his book, *Paris Enchanted*, Bidermanas came to London to take the photographs for *Gala Day London*, published in 1953. Conceived in poetic terms, each photograph in the book is accompanied by a specially composed piece by a leading poet or writer of the time. The photographs shown here are taken from the book, and are reproduced together with the original poem.

IZIS BIDERMANAS (1911–1980)

Tired Sailor, Piccadilly Circus, c. 1953

Reproduced from Gala Day London

The surgery of light clinks and hoots to a stop the switchback evening. Coloured periscopes probe asphalt canals where taxis cruise and park their cat's eyes. Litter drifts over stone islands, seaweed of cigarette ends, an octopus of news. Neon moons, sun balloons, bonnets of cars like patent leather and a panic of changing signals on a zealous shoe tap out his zodiac.

The first sleep over a Good Conduct stripe takes the edge off misery, the usual let-down. Everything gets flatter, the composite ego deflating. Public bars were, in a way, harbours, but nothing can muffle the clank of the milk train skimming the dawn off Portsmouth and anyhow a cap, naming its ship in letters of pale gold, will have to be accounted for.

Alan Ross (poet and critic)

Man Blowing Bubbles, Petticoat Lane, c. 1953

Reproduced from Gala Day London

Bubbles made with soap, and a little grid of iron and off into the
air they go like spoken thoughts.

Henry Green (novelist)

HENRI CARTIER-BRESSON (b.1908)

for biographical notes see page 161

London Suburbs, 1954

Modern Silver print. Magnum Photos

Cartier-Bresson's best-known photographs feature people caught by the camera at what he called 'the decisive moment'. However, as this photograph suggests, his full range of work was more varied. The precise location of this view is not recorded, but that is not important because the photograph conveys so eloquently the density of the endless acres of suburban housing which covered much of Greater London.

Newspaper Seller and City Businessman, c. 1955

Modern Silver print. Magnum Photos

Cartier-Bresson's photographs of everyday life in London in the 1950s are less well-known than some of his other work, but they are amongst the most telling pictures of the period.

AYNE came to live in London in 1954 and worked as a freelance photographer. Interested in both painting and photography, he was a supporter of the 'new realism' in art then being championed by, amongst others, John Berger, and was an admirer of the snapshot aesthetic as practised, for example, by Henri Cartier-Bresson. In the late 1950s and early 1960s Mayne carried out a long-term project in North Kensington, the area where he lived, based on the idea of documenting ordinary people, especially the young, as they carried out their lives on the street. According to his wife, the playwright and theatre director, Ann Jellicoe: *'Photography became the means, motive, point of Roger's life. Through photography he lived, justified himself, made contact with others and began to release the aggression generated in his [repressed] childhood.'* (Mayne, 1986, page 70).

ROGER MAYNE (b.1929)

Gambling Group, Southam Street, North Kensington, 1958

Modern silver print. Museum of London (IN15269)

Few of Mayne's pictures are posed and his technique for achieving 'invisibility' was not to hide his camera, as Paul Martin had done, but to make himself such a familiar figure that people became oblivious to his presence.

Off the Harrow Road, Paddington, 1955

Modern silver print. Museum of London (IN15278)

Here the broken-down fence and temporary prefabricated houses, a legacy of the Second World War, signify the transitional status of this part of North Kensington, which was comprehensively redeveloped a few years after the photograph was taken.

208

Boy Trying to Catch a Football, Brindley Road, Paddington, 1956

Modern silver print. Museum of London (IN15275)

S MITH trained in London as an architect in the early 1930s and then became a freelance photographer with a special interest in architecture and landscape. After the War he established an outstanding reputation for providing illustrations for books and magazines on English architectural and landscape themes.

EDWIN SMITH (1912–1971)

Soldiers Marching, St. James's Palace, c. 1960

Silver print. Museum of London (IN7690)

Most of Smith's photographs are architectural or landscape studies, but this rare picture taken in London during a snowstorm shows his versatility.

London Bridge from Fishmongers Hall, c. 1957

Silver print. Museum of London (IN7658)

This is one of a series of photographs Smith took for the book, *The Living City,* which was published by the Corporation of London in 1957. Smith's brief was to show the blend of modernity and tradition in the City, and many of the pictures show just the sort of juxtaposition we see here.

A House in St. John's Wood, c. 1955

Silver print. Museum of London (IN7743)

During the 1950s and 1960s Smith made a number of pictures in London which feature suburban houses.

Mending a Car and Motor Scooter, Alton Estate, Roehampton, c. 1955

Silver print. Museum of London (IN7748)

Built by the LCC after the Second World War, Alton Estate was meant to be a show-piece of what could be achieved in public housing. It was situated on the edge of Richmond Park and demonstrated the LCC's commitment to providing 'affordable' accommodation in some of the more attractive parts of London. The eleven-storey blocks were designed according to principles developed before the Second World War by Le Corbusier.

Bankside, c. 1960

Silver print. Museum of London (IN7639)

In the 1960s the Thames began to look desolate as more and more of the old wharves lost business to the down-stream, deep-water wharves and enclosed docks which could handle the larger modern vessels. Smith's poignant positioning of the swans against the backdrop of derelict warehouses heightens the sense of human abandonment.

C OLLINS began working as a photojournalist in 1956 and his photographs were widely published. He was also a prolific writer on photographic matters, on travel and on the English countryside. In 1995 he is still photographing for various gardening magazines.

BOB COLLINS (b. 1924)

'Rush Hour' at Victoria Station, c. 1960

Modern silver print. Museum of London (IN15976)

URING the 1960s, Gifford set about photographing the last days of steam on British railways, and in so doing he helped to redefine the scope of railway photography. Until then railway photographers had been largely content with making portraits of locomotives. Gifford, however, looked at the whole of the railway environment, particularly in its urban and industrial setting, and adopted a photographic approach which captured the atmosphere of the scene. His book, *Decline of Steam*, caused something of a sensation in railway photography circles when it first appeared in 1965.

COLIN T. GIFFORD (b.?)

Inside Old Oak Common Roundhouse, 26 April 1962

Silver print. Museum of London (IN15893)

Since most of Britian's mainline railways terminate in London, it is not surprising that several major locomotive and carriage maintenance depots were built in the capital. In fact, in those parts of London where such facilities were established, the railway often became the main employer in the area. Old Oak Common Depot in North Acton was built to serve the Great Western Railway's mainline into Paddington. This photograph was used in Gifford's second book, *Each a Glimpse*, published in 1970.

Entrance to St. Pancras Station, c. 1965

Silver print. Museum of London (IN15894)

The British railway network was modernised in the 1960s in a programme which included the replacement of steam engines with diesel and electric locomotives. Gifford's ambitious project to document the last years of steam on British railways led him to London where he photographed many locations, including most of the mainline termini.

AFTER living in South Africa for several years, Goldblatt returned to London in 1962 and obtained a job as an advertising copywriter. In the mid-1960s, however, he gave this up and started working as a freelance documentary photographer, mainly for national Sunday newspaper magazines. This continued into the mid-1990s except for the period between 1988 and 1992 when he was picture editor for the environmental organisation, Greenpeace.

JOHN GOLDBLATT (b. 1930)

Houses of Parliament Viewed from Vauxhall, 1964
Silver print. John Goldblatt

Father and Son Raising Sprouts Near the Royal Victoria Dock, 1966
Silver print. John Goldblatt

HURN took up photography in 1955 and was briefly employed by the Reflex agency before he turned freelance and worked for various magazines, including *Look*, *Life* and the *Sunday Times Magazine*. He was elected a member of Magnum Photos in 1967. In the early 1970s, he set up the highly respected course in Documentary Photography at Gwent College of Higher Education in Newport, South Wales.

DAVID HURN (b.1934)

A Stripper's Dressing Room, Soho, 1965

Silver print. Magnum Photos

London's sex industry became much more visible on the streets of Soho during the so-called 'Swinging Sixties'. Hurn documented activity behind the scenes to reveal the banality beneath the surface glamour.

LIEBLING, an American, spent a year living and working in London in 1967. Already noted for his photography in America, where he was an executive officer of The Photo League in New York City, he produced an extensive series of social documentary photographs of all types of Londoners going about their everyday business.

JEROME LIEBLING (b.1924)

Youths in Enfield Park, 1967

Modern silver print. Museum of London (IN15560)

Outside Claridge's Hotel, 1967

Modern silver print. Museum of London (IN15553)

The social contrasts to be found in London has been a recurring theme in documentary photography.

222

FTER studying Graphic Design at the London School (later College) of Printing, Ray-Jones went to America to complete his studies. He became interested in photography and, in 1963, attended classes at the Design Laboratory run by Alexey Brodovitch in New York in order to develop his skills. The Design Laboratory was very influential at this time and was the training ground for a number of successful photographers. Ray-Jones returned to England in 1966 with plans to produce a book. To this end he documented English culture until, in 1971, he went back to America to teach. Sadly, he became ill and died of leukemia in 1972. Although he did not take a great many photographs in London, some of his best pictures were taken there. His English work was published posthumously in the book, *A Day Off: An English Journal*, in 1974, and influenced a new generation of British documentary photographers who were searching for a fresh approach.

TONY RAY-JONES (1924–1972)

Wimbledon, 1968

Silver print. John Benton-Harris

S PENCER ran an aerial photography business until 1952 when he joined *Life* magazine as a photojournalist specialising in stories on Africa and South East Asia. In 1972 he became a freelancer working for various magazines, including *Time* and *Paris Match*.

TERRY SPENCER (b.1918)

A Gang of Skinheads Passing a Group of Hippies, Piccadilly Circus, 1969

Silver print. Museum of London (IN7444)

Gang of 'Mod' Youths, Borehamwood, 1969

Silver print. Museum of London (IN7434)

The adoption of a distinctive style of dress, almost a uniform, to signify membership of a particular social group, became a familiar feature of post-War youth culture. Spencer took a series of photographs exploring this theme for *Life* magazine during the 1960s.

1970 – 1994

G AY was a professional photographer whose commercial work was mainly in advertising, where he specialised in photographing animals. He also worked as an architectural photographer, and published several books, including *London's Historic Railway Stations* (1972), which was produced jointly with Sir John Betjeman. The photographs shown here are taken from this book.

JOHN GAY (b.?)

Liverpool St. Station, c. 1972
Silver print. John Gay

'Let gothic lancets spring and soar and iron ribs disclose the sky'.

Sir John Betjeman (1972)

From Blackfriars Railway Bridge Looking Towards Southwark Bridge, c. 1972

Silver print. John Gay

By the 1970s the river Thames, once the capital's busiest highway, had fallen into almost complete disuse as a result of the closure of the up-river wharves and docks.

N the 1970s Perry took a series of photographs to show what Londoners did during their spare time.

ROGER PERRY (b. ?)

'Teds' Outside the Black Raven Pub, Bishopsgate, City of London, c. 1972

Silver print. Museum of London (IN7798)

The 'Teddy Boy' style popular in the 1950s enjoyed something of a revival in the 1970s.

The 'Rolling Stones' in Concert, Earl's Court, c. 1976

Silver print. Museum of London (IN7807)

230

FTER training as a painter, McCullin completed his National Service from 1953 to 1955 as a Photographic Assistant with the RAF. He began working as a freelance photojournalist in 1961, and then under contract to the *Sunday Times* from 1964. He achieved an international reputation for his photographs of the battlefields of Vietnam and elsewhere, and his graphic but compassionate images, which were featured in the Sunday newspaper colour supplements, marked a new attitude towards war photography. In the early 1970s he returned to England to photograph, and documented, amongst other things, those battling for survival in the face of extreme poverty. He joined Magnum Photos in 1984.

DON McCULLIN (b.1935)

Near Spitalfields Market, 1973

Silver print. Magnum Photos

Many of McCullin's documentary photographs of England in the 1970s were taken in the de-industrialising North, but London, his home town, was where he found some of the most destitute people.

A SWISS-BORN freelance photojournalist, Mayer worked for numerous newspapers and magazines and had, by 1994, published over thirty books of his photographs. His work was distributed by Magnum Photos from 1969 onwards.

FRED MAYER (b.1933)

Eros at Night, 1974

Colour transparency. Magnum Photos

Mayer produced this image by sandwiching together two separate transparencies, one of the statue of Eros in silhouette, and the other of the background lights. The effect is impressive.

T REVOR was a freelance documentary photographer and filmmaker who helped to found the Half Moon Photography Workshop, later Camerawork, in the early 1970s. He subsequently contributed photographs to several important publications and exhibitions, and from 1973 to 1993 he worked on an extensive personal project, called 'Eastender', which was an in-depth study of the multi-ethnic community centred around Brick Lane in the East End of London. This was Trevor's own neighbourhood, and he recorded a community struggling to survive in the face of large-scale urban redevelopment, racist aggression and changing social values. In 1990 an archive of 300 photographs from the project was purchased by the Museum of London.

PAUL TREVOR (b. 1947)

Kids Playing, Fournier Street, E1, 1974

Silver print. Museum of London (IN16030)

Textile Sweatshop, Fournier Street, E1, 1979

Silver print. Museum of London (IN16042)

Whitechapel has long been a centre for textile production, and became notorious in the nineteenth century for its sweatshops which employed cheap, often immigrant Jewish, labour. The system persisted in the late twentieth century with labour provided by Bangladeshi immigrants.

Lolesworth Close, Commercial Street, E1, 1978

Silver print. Museum of London (IN16039)

This view typifies the apalling state of parts of the East End before the building boom of the 1980s. For years the authorities had prevaricated over how to plan the redevelopment of the East End, but ultimately it was largely handed over to the piecemeal efforts of private developers for whom the property market was the only real client.

Boy with Toy Gun, Brick Lane, E1, 1978

Silver print. Museum of London (IN16029)

Trevor's project can be compared to Roger Mayne's study of North Kensington in the 1950s. *See page 207.*

Girl in the Rain, Chilton Street, E2, 1977

Silver print. Museum of London (IN16026)

237

B ENTON-HARRIS was born in New York City and attended classes at Alexey Brodovitch's influential Design Laboratory in 1961–1962. After a period with the US Army in Italy, he settled in England in 1965 and began to work as a photographer, and later also as a part-time teacher and exhibition curator. He began a long-term personal project to document the nature of the English character in 1965, and this was still underway in the early 1990s. Many of the pictures, especially those from the 1970s, were taken in the London area and the work, which can be described as a kind of 'visual sociology', represents one of the most comprehensive photographic studies of its kind. Benton-Harris has exhibited and taught in both Britain and America.

JOHN BENTON-HARRIS (b. 1939)

Derby Day, 1976

Silver print. John Benton-Harris

Like others before him, notably Horace Nicholls (*see page 103 and 113*), Benton-Harris regarded the annual sporting events which comprised the London Season as rewarding occasions for studying the English character, especially that of the upper classes.

Charing Cross Road, 1974

Silver print. John Benton-Harris

During the 1970s Benton-Harris found many of his subjects on the streets of London. He was one of several photographers who felt that by the early 1990s, however, there were fewer subjects of interest to be found there.

The Wedding of Prince Charles and Lady Diana Spencer, 1981

Colour transparencies. John Benton-Harris

'Charles and Di's Wedding' was a big media event. Benton-Harris was offered several lucrative commissions to photograph the Royal couple as they passed by some predetermined point, but he eschewed these in favour of a roving brief which would allow him to photograph the spectators instead. These pictures were taken on the night before the wedding.

ORN in England, Berry moved to South Africa in 1952 where he lived and worked as a photojournalist before returning to England in the late 1960s, having been elected a member of the prestigious Magnum Photos agency in 1963. In 1974 he became the first photographer to receive a major bursary from the Arts Council of Great Britain, which enabled him to carry out a personal exploration of England and the English way of life. Most of the photographs were taken during 1975 and a selection of them, including those shown here, was published in 1978 in *The English*, which can be seen as a sequel to Bill Brandt's 1936 book, *The English At Home*.

IAN BERRY (b. 1935)

Doctor's Waiting Room, Battersea, c. 1975
Silver print. Magnum Photos

Man eating in the Street, Spitalfields, c. 1975
Silver print. Magnum Photos

Since the beginning of the century, photographers concerned with poverty in London have focused on the East End, especially the area around Spitalfields Market.

Hyde Park, c. 1975

Silver print. Magnum Photos

It is evident that in the forty years or so between Bill Brandt's study of the social fabric of London *(see pages 156 and 167)* and Berry's similar investigation, the gap between the rich and the poor had not diminished.

244

Couple Kissing, New Year's Eve, Trafalgar Square, c. 1975

Silver print. Magnum Photos

In the foreword to his book, *The English* (1978), Berry remarked on the fact that England did not seem to have changed much in the years he had been away. After his experiences photographing in South Africa he was able to record that he found England to be *'...the easiest country in the world in which to take photographs – in the way people react or rather do not react in the photographer's presence'*.

A S an amateur photographer, Fear completed a project on the theme of *Weekend London*, which won her the first ever Nikon Scholarship in 1975. In 1978 photographs from the project were exhibited at the South Bank, and in the same year she became a freelance professional photographer working for various Sunday and current affairs magazines.

SALLY FEAR (b.1947)

Chinese New Year Celebrations, Gerrard Street, Soho, 1976

Modern silver print. Museum of London (IN15802)

246

I N 1978, with funding provided by the Arts Council of Great Britain, the Museum of London commissioned Lewis, a freelance documentary photographer who had obtained an MA in Photography from the Royal College of Art in 1975, to take a series of photographs on the theme of commuting. The results were exhibited at the Museum in 1978 under the title, *Coming and Going.*

BARRY LEWIS (b.?)

Charing Cross Station, 5.30pm, 1978

Silver print. Museum of London (IN8208)

RICE'S photographic career began as an assistant to the studio-based fashion and beauty photographer Peter Deal. He became a freelancer in the early 1980s and began to specialise in location work, mainly portrait and editorial photography for magazines. As a Londoner born and bred, Rice has photographed the capital continuously since the 1970s.

JIM RICE (b. 1949)

Couple on a Bench, Tower of London, 1979
Silver print. Museum of London (IN7168)

TV Crew at a National Front Rally, Walworth, 1980

Silver print. Museum of London (IN7161)

Rice has a good eye for unusual or amusing situations. His candid street photographs are telling observations of everyday London life.

Van Driver, Deptford Creek, 1993

Silver print. Jim Rice

250

Eddie Stabling his Horse, Stowage, Deptford Creek, 1993

Silver print. Jim Rice

During the early 1990s Rice carried out an extensive project to document the industrialised area around Deptford Creek before redevelopment. A book of the photographs, *Deptford Creek*, was published in 1993.

RIGINALLY trained as an architect and painter, Evans turned to photography in 1977. His particular concern as a photographer was to explore the concept of 'urban landscape', seeing the environment both as the expression of human activity in the past and as a framework that shapes activities in the present. During the 1980s and early 1990s he carried out several projects in Docklands and the City of London whilst these areas were undergoing major redevelopment.

TOM EVANS (b. 1948)

King George V Dock, 1979

Silver print. Museum of London (IN7853)

By the end of the 1970s London's docks, with the exception of Tilbury, had closed to shipping. Until the creation of the London Docklands Development Corporation in 1981, much of the riverside and dockland areas lay derelict and their future was the subject of debate. Evans was one of the few photographers to realise that whatever happened, the changes would have an enormous impact on the docklands landscape, and that the area should be recorded before the developers moved in.

Wood Street, City of London, 1990

Silver print. Museum of London (IN15534)

The building boom of the 1980s caused dramatic changes to the fabric of the City of London. In functional terms there are distinct parallels to be drawn between this period and the latter part of the nineteenth century. In both cases large-scale redevelopment of the City was undertaken primarily as a response to the demands of new technology, thus ensuring the continuing role of the City as a leading World financial centre. Evans's photograph was taken during the construction of Albangate, designed by Terrence Farrell, which was built across London Wall. In front of it stands the tower of St. Alban's, the rest of the church having been destroyed during the Second World War.

N admirer of the work of nineteenth- and early twentieth-century topographical photographers, notably the Parisian view-makers, Charles Marville and Eugene Atget, Barkshire learned how to use a large-format camera and, in 1978, embarked upon an ambitious project to create a comprehensive topographical record of London. This led him to carry his 10" x 8" view camera to practically every part of the capital, and though many of the resulting photographs are of well-preserved historic buildings and monuments, others show a broader view of London's built environment, including less distinguished streets and buildings and those threatened with destruction.

PAUL BARKSHIRE (b. 1953)

Hay's Wharf, 1985

Silver print. Paul Barkshire

By the mid-1980s the redevelopment of many central riverside wharves was well underway. Factories and warehouses were replaced by offices and apartments, often created by converting the original industrial buildings. This view shows the transition of Hay's Wharf taking place behind the slogan, 'The outlook is getting brighter every day'.

Whitechapel Road, 1981

Silver print. Museum of London (IN14188)

This view says much about the decline of the East End following the closure of the docks and the de-industrialisation of London in the 1970s and 1980s.

Workshop, Meard Street, Soho, 17 March 1981

Silver print. Museum of London (IN8340)

In the context of the decline of Britain's manufacturing industry, this traditional-looking workshop has the air of a museum display. In fact, what was once the most common form of manufacturing site in London – the workshop – is now undergoing a modest revival as part of the growth of the heritage industry.

SELF-TAUGHT photojournalist, Marlow joined the Sygma photo agency in 1977 and worked for various international magazines, including *Time*, *Newsweek*, *Sunday Times Magazine*, *Stern*, and *Paris Match*. He left Sygma in 1980 and became an associate member of Magnum Photos in 1982, then a full member in 1986.

PETER MARLOW (b.1952)

Footbridge and Warehouse, Millwall Dock, 1982

Silver print. Magnum Photos

Marlow was one of the photographers chosen by the Photographers' Gallery to participate in its 1982 'London Project'. He produced a series of landscape views of the Isle of Dogs at night which depict the dereliction of the area prior to its redevelopment later in the decade.

TRAINED originally as an illustrator, Taylor studied photography at the Royal College of Art where his main interest was in social documentary photography. In 1982, however, he took the photograph which is reproduced here and started to become interested in topographical subject matter and a more objective approach. He photographed extensively in the suburban area where he lived in North London. In 1989 he published a book, *Ideal Home*, which contained photographs taken in and around one particular middle-class suburban house.

JOHN R. J. TAYLOR

North London Suburbia, 1982

Silver print. Museum of London (IN15562)

Here is the substance to confirm the stereotype of the 'good life' as lived in London's leafy, middle-class, inter-war suburbs. It is interesting to compare this photograph with Cartier-Bresson's 1950s' view of an older working-class London suburb. *See page 205.*

GARANTH SOCKI (b. ?)

Bexleyheath, 1985

Colour coupler print. Museum of London (IN15682)

This is one of a series of views taken in South-East London and North Kent by Socki for his photography degree. His aim was to show the environmental and social impact of de-industrialisation in what had become, by the mid-1980s, a very depressed region. In the 1990s, government policy encouraged private investment in these parts of East London, North Kent and Essex, which became known collectively as the 'East Thames Corridor'.

ORN in Holland, Matze began working as a photo-journalist in 1970. She settled in London in 1982, and obtained a degree in Photography at the University of Westminster. She subsequently worked as an architectural and commercial photographer, and as a part-time teacher and exhibition organiser. As a personal project, which she began shortly after she came to London, Matze photographed in Kensal Green Cemetery, concentrating at first on the Victorian landscape and then on the ritual of the burial ceremony.

YOKE MATZE (b.1945)

Black Funeral, Kensal Green Cemetery, c. 1985

Silver print. Museum of London (IN14805)

Part of Matze's project on Kensal Green Cemetery was to document the burial ceremony as practised by people from different cultural and ethnic backgrounds.

Kensal Green Cemetery, Harrow Road, W10, c. 1985

Silver print. Museum of London (IN14802)

Kensal Green Cemetery, which was opened in 1833, was the first of seven commercial cemeteries established in London during the nineteenth century by The General Cemetery Company. Many famous people are buried there, including the great engineers, Mark Isambard Brunel and his son, Isambard Kingdom Brunel (*see pages 42 and 43*). The landscape of the cemetery is full of fascinating forms and Matze photographed these with great sensitivity. Snow adds its own, almost surreal quality to this view of one of the main avenues.

W ROBLEWSKI specialises in documenting the art of the tattooist.

CHRIS WROBLEWSKI (b. ?)

South London Skinhead, c.1985

Silver print. Museum of London (IN15727)

This photograph is from a series of tattooed Londoners published in Wroblewski's book, *City Indians* (1983), which explored the role of body decoration in youth culture in the early 1980s.

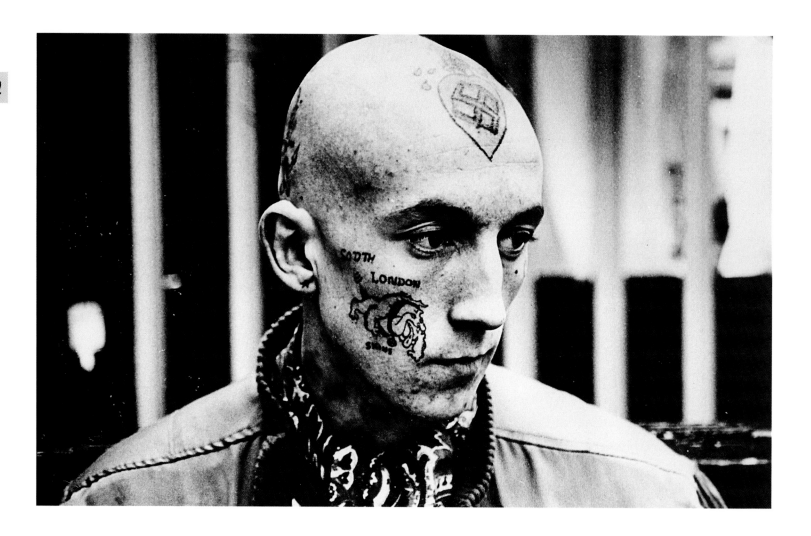

WHILST studying for a part-time degree in photography at the Polytechnic of Central London (later the University of Westminster), Tapper, a professional medical photographer, took a series of street photographs illustrating 'a walk through the East End'. The pictures highlight the strong Asian presence in an area which, because of its proximity to the docks, has a long history of immigrant settlement.

BOB TAPPER (b.1953)

Whitechapel High Street, 1986

Colour coupler print. Museum of London (IN15749)

AFTER graduating in Photography in 1981, Friedman became a commercial photographer and illustrator who specialised in producing record covers and book jackets, sometimes using new digital imaging techniques alongside traditional photographic processes.

JIM FRIEDMAN (b. 1959)

Panorama of Piccadilly Circus, 1988

Cibachrome print. Museum of London (IN15574)

Friedman took this photograph with a swing-lens panoramic camera and created the impressionistic effect by moving the camera during the exposure. The result is a refreshingly modern approach towards the pictorialist's goal of producing images which convey feeling rather than information.

F OX graduated in Photography at West Surrey College of Art and Design in 1986. In 1987 the Museum of London and Camerawork commissioned her to take a series of photographs documenting office life in London during the 'Thatcher Years', and a selection of the resulting photographs was exhibited and published by Camerawork under the title, *Workstations*, in 1988.

ANNA FOX (b. 1961)

Female Office Worker, 1987

Colour coupler print. Museum of London (IN15577)

During the late 1980s the office computer revolution was well under way and this was allied to the adoption of new attitudes and business practices related to the political climate.

Salesmen in a City Pub, 1987

Colour coupler print. Museum of London (IN15578)

EGINNING in the late 1980s and continuing into the 1990s, Delaney, an architectural photographer, was engaged in a project to photograph by night London's varied and changing urban landscape. As well as photographing for himself, he also tried whenever possible to fulfill his commercial assignments by photographing at night. His book, *London After Dark*, was published in 1993. Many of the pictures record the major redevelopments which were taking place, including the transformation of Canary Wharf on the Isle of Dogs into a high-tech business district, but he was equally interested in photographing other, less spectacular parts of London, often revealing them, literally, in a new light.

ALAN DELANEY (b. 1958)

Martello Street, London Fields, E8, 1989

Silver print. Museum of London (IN15860)

A side street underneath a railway bridge in Hackney which was a temporary site for a group of travellers. There are no fields in London Fields.

Annett's Crescent, Essex Road, N1, 1989

Silver print. Museum of London (IN15858)

Early nineteenth-century suburban houses divided into studio apartments in gentrified Islington.

Canary Wharf, Isle of Dogs, 1991

Silver print. Museum of London (IN15857)

With its controversial tower, one of the tallest buildings in Europe, designed by Cesar Pelli, Canary Wharf was the flagship of the 1980s redevelopment boom, and symbolised the domination of business interests in public affairs which became a hallmark of British politics during this period.

AS part of its 1988 'London Project', the Photographers' Gallery commissioned Daly to photograph on the theme of *Monopoly*, the popular game invented in Philadelphia in the early 1930s by Charles Darrow. He made a series of views of the London streets which feature in the game, contrasting modern reality with the outdated image of London which it perpetuates.

TIM DALY (b. 1964)

Fleet Street, 1988

Colour coupler print. Museum of London (IN15691)

Until the late 1980s, Fleet Street was dominated by the newspaper and printing industries which had been located there for several centuries. By 1995 these industries had almost completely left Central London for other locations, notably in Docklands, where new technology could be more easily implemented.

COOK is a self-taught, semi-professional architectural and landscape photographer. Between 1989 and 1991 he carried out a personal project to document the streets and buildings of the City of London at night. This was inspired by the series of night-time photographs of Paris taken by Brassaï in the 1930s.

ANDY COOK (b. 1960)

Looking North from Philpot Lane, City of London, 11.57pm, c. 1990

Colour transparency. Andy Cook

The view is towards the Lloyds Building, on the left, and the area around St. Mary Axe which was being rebuilt after sustaining severe damage from an IRA car-bomb.

D ORLEY-BROWN, a freelance photographer based in East London, spent several months in 1988 as photographer-in-residence at Homerton Hospital in Hackney. As part of this project, commissioned by Homerton Hospital's Arts Committee and The Public Arts Development Trust, he documented the range of healthcare services provided by the hospital to create a photographic archive for the North East Thames Regional Health Authority.

CHRIS DORLEY-BROWN (b. 1958)

X-ray Patient, Homerton Hospital, Hackney, 1988

Colour coupler print. Museum of London (IN15631)

One of the themes Dorley-Brown explored was the feeling of unease which many patients experience when confronted with the sophisticated technology of a modern hospital.

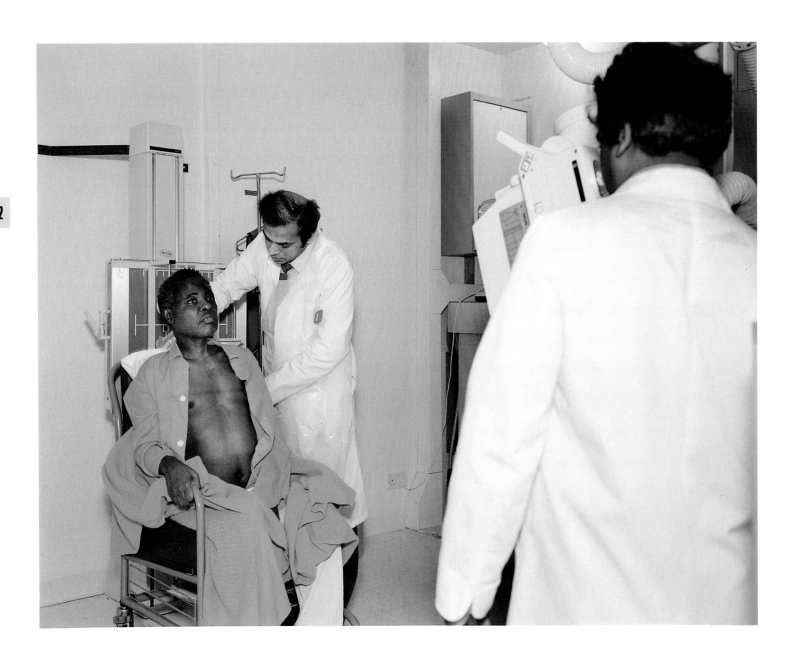

ED BARBER (b. ?)

Bill and Dolly Luff, Loraine Estate, Holloway, c. 1989

Silver print. Museum of London (IN15484)

On behalf of Islington Borough Council, Barber photographed a selection of people who lived or worked in the borough in order to publicise the work of the Council in the areas of housing, employment and social welfare. The Council's Press, Campaign and Publicity Unit mounted an exhibition of the photographs and published them in the book, *Islington's People*.

AFTER leaving school in 1975 Segal became a photographer's assistant. She then embarked on a career as a freelance portrait and editorial photographer and in 1990 she won the *Observer Magazine*'s Jane Bown Portrait Award. In 1993 the Museum of London commissioned her to complete a series of contemporary portraits of Londoners at home, and these were exhibited at the Museum in 1993–1994 to complement historical investigation by the Museum into the origins of London's multicultural population.

MAGDA SEGAL (b.1959)

Single Mother with her Children, Camberwell, SE5, 1991

Silver print. Museum of London (IN16017)

274

Lubavitch Hassidic Family, Stamford Hill, 1993

Silver print. Museum of London (IN16016)

Segal's project on Londoners at home combined the portrayal of a range of people from different ethnic backgrounds with the representation of their individual lifestyles as revealed by the interiors of their homes. A book of Segal's photographs, *London at Home*, was published in 1994.

HAVING trained originally as a painter and sculptor, Cardwell taught for several years before becoming a freelance photographer in 1980. He was a regular contributor to the *Guardian* and *Independent* newspapers and also carried out a number of personal projects. Several of these were concerned with documenting the lives of different communities in London, especially in the East End.

KEITH CARDWELL (b. 1946)

Sunday Market, Cheshire Street, E2, 1991

Silver print. Museum of London

Much of Cardwell's street photography in the early 1990s was carried out in Spitalfields in East London. He favours photographing his subjects close-up using a 35mm camera with an ultra-wide angle lens.

AFTER training in fine art, Baldesare spent several years working as a staff photographer for an advertising company. In 1984 he turned freelance and in between commercial assignments carried out several of his own social documentary projects during the 1980s and early 1990s.

PAUL BALDESARE (b. 1953)

Early Morning Commuter, London Metropolitan Line, 1994

Colour coupler print. Paul Baldesare

One of Baldesare's projects was a long-term study of passengers on the London underground, which was carried out first in black and white and then in colour. The photographs were mostly taken without raising the camera to the eye so that the subject was not aware of being photographed.

S EABORNE began photographing in London in 1979 following his appointment as Curator of the Historic Photographs Collection at the Museum of London. After completing a series of documentary photographs of the Isle of Dogs during the early years of redevelopment there from 1981 to 1986, he began on a long-term landscape project to record deindustrial-isation, changing patterns of land use and the the provision of new transport infrastructure.

MIKE SEABORNE (b.1954)

Demolition of Deptford Power Station, April 1992

Colour coupler print. Museum of London

London's twentieth-century industrial might was symbolised by the string of power stations which were built along the banks of the Thames in the 1930s. All but one of these (Lots Road, which generates electricity for the London Underground) have now closed, and some have been demolished. A luxury hotel and marina were among the proposals for the development of the site of Deptford Power Station.

The best future for Britain.

Docklands Light Railway, Limeharbour, Isle of Dogs, September 1987

Colour coupler print. Museum of London

The Docklands Light Railway from Tower Hill to Island Gardens was formally opened by Her Majesty the Queen on 30 July 1987, but was not opened to the public until 31 August. Seaborne recorded the new railway during the first few months of its operation, combining social documentary with landscape photography.

TRAINER was a film animator who, in the early 1990s, undertook personal photographic projects in his spare time. His primary interest was in making documentary portraits and his work in London included a series of photographs of travellers and another of football supporters.

DAVID TRAINER (b. 1954)

Beggar, Oxford Circus Underground Station, 1994
Silver print. David Trainer

Travellers, Epsom Fair, June 1994

Silver print. David Trainer

ARGELY self-taught as a photographer, Marshall carried out numerous documentary and urban landscape projects on London themes during the 1980s and early 1990s, the results of which were frequently exhibited.

PETER MARSHALL (b.1945)

Panoramic View of Carter Lane, EC4, 1992
Colour coupler print. Peter Marshall

Panoramic View of the Docklands Light Railway Beckton Extension Under Construction, 1992
Silver print. Peter Marshall

The Docklands Light Railway extension from Poplar to Beckton was opened in 1994. This photograph was taken at the point where the railway crosses the River Lea at Canning Town, and is one of a series from a personal project undertaken by Marshall to record the line whilst under construction. The panoramic format reinforces the railway's essentially linear nature, and the curvilinear distortion associated with the type of swing-lens panoramic camera used by Marshall echoes the curvature of the railway arches and of the river.

TOM HUNTER (b.1965) AND
JAMES MACKINNON (b.1968)

London Fields – The Ghetto, 1994

3-D photographic sculpture. Museum of London

'The Ghetto' is the result of a collaboration between Hunter, a photographer, and Mackinnon, a modelmaker. It documents the homes and lifestyles of a community of squatters who occupied two parallel side streets off Mare Street in Hackney and which was under threat from the redevelopment of the area by the local Council. The project was undertaken by Hunter, a member of the community, as part of his photography degree at the London College of Printing. As well as documenting the area before demolition, he wished, in the face of impending legislation to make squatting illegal, to represent the community in a positive way.

The exterior photographs were taken with a large-format view camera and colour prints were made to scale. The interiors were made from 35mm prints collaged to create a three-dimensional effect. Hunter also produced a set of portraits of individual squatters in their rooms which was inspired, he says, by the work of Dutch painters in the seventeenth century, especially that of Johannes Vermeer.

APPENDICES

List of Photographers

List of Illustrations and Picture Acknowledgements

Bibliography

Index

LIST OF PHOTOGRAPHERS

SURNAME	FORENAME (S)	PAGE (S)
Arapoff	Cyril	22, 150–55
Avery	John H.	20, 92–4, 110–11
Baldesare	Paul	277
Barber	Ed	273
Barkshire	Paul	254–56
Benton-Harris	John	238–41
Berry	Ian	242–45
Bevington	Geoffrey	48–9
Bidermanas	Izis	202–04
Blake	A.H.	143
Blanchard	Valentine	16, 47–8
Bool	Alfred and John	63–4
Brandt	Bill	22, 156–60, 167–69
Broom	Christina	100–01
Campbell-Gray		98–9
Cardwell	Keith	276
Cartier-Bresson	Henri	161, 205–06
Casparious	Hans	130
Cembrano	F. P.	79
Coburn	Alvin Langdon	20, 95–7
Collins	Bob	215
Cook	Andy	271
Cross & Tibbs	Arthur & Fred	24, 170–73
Daly	Tim	270
Davison	George	89
Delaney	Alan	28, 267–69
Dixon	Henry	18, 56–7, 70–2
Dixon-Scott	John	124
Dorley-Brown	Chris	272
Evans	Tom	252–53
Fear	Sally	246
Fenton	Roger	44–5
Flather	Henry	50–1
Fox	Anna	266
Friedman	Jim	264–65
Galt	Rev. John	20, 86–8

288

SURNAME	FORENAME (S)	PAGE (S)	SURNAME	FORENAME (S)	PAGE (S)
Gay	John	228–29	Mortimer	Francis James	112
Gifford	Colin T.	216–17	Murch	Horace A.	142, jacket
Goldblatt	John	218–19	Nicholls	Horace W.	20, 103–04, 113–15
Grant	Henry	196–99	Perry	Roger	230–01
Griggs	Noel	162	Prout	Victor	48
Hardy	Bert	24, 180–82, 190–93	Ransome	A. J.	82
Harker	Margaret	200	Ray-Jones	Tony	26, 223
Hedderly	James	61	Reid	George Davison	125–29
Henderson	Nigel	195	Rice	Jim	28, 248–51
Hopkins	Thurston	188–89	Rodger	George	24, 176–77
Hoppé	Emil Otto	131–33	Rosling	Alfred	39
Howlett	Robert	42–3	Sanford	John	60
Hunter &	Tom &		Seaborne	Mike	278–79
Mackinnon	James	28, 284–85	Segal	Magda	274–75
Hurn	David	220	Shadbolt	George	16,46
Jarché	James	119	Sinclair	James	105
Job	Charles	120–21	Smith	Edwin	210–14
Judge	Fred	118	Smyth	Norah	106–07
Kersting	Anthony	163	Socki	Garanth	259
Kilburn	William	38	Speller	Reggie	183
Lemere	Bedford	73	Spencer	Terry	224–25
Lewis	Barry	247	Spender	Humphrey	138–39
Liebling	Jerome	26, 221–22	St. Croix	M. de	34–35
Man	Felix H.	22, 140–41	Stone	John H.	194
Marlow	Peter	257	Strudwick	William	52–5
Marshall	Peter	282–83	Stuart	Francis G. O.	75
Martin	Paul	18, 80–2	Suschitzky	Wolfgang	144–46
Mason	Herbert	166	Talbot	William Henry Fox	16, 36–7
Matze	Yoke	260–61	Tapper	Bob	263
Mayer	Fred	233	Taylor	John R.J.	258
Mayne	Roger	26, 207–09	Thomson	John	18, 67–9
McCullin	Don	232	Trainer	David	280–81
Miles & Kay		108–09	Trevor	Paul	28, 234–37
Monck	Margaret	147–49	Whiffin	William	102, 122–23, 201
Montizon	Count de	40	Wilson	Charles A.	76–78
Morgan & Laing		65	Wroblewski	Chris	262

LIST OF ILLUSTRATIONS AND PICTURE ACKNOWLEDGEMENTS

Every effort has been made to contact the original copyright holders. The publishers would be pleased to make good any errors or omissions brought to our attention in future editions.

M. de St. Croix, Whitehall from Trafalgar Square, September/October, 1839, Victoria & Albert Museum (1-1986); **W.H.F. Talbot**, Trafalgar Square and Nelson's Column, 1843, NMPFT (1937-3943)/Science & Society Picture Library; Hungerford Suspension Bridge, from the North Bank Looking South, c. 1845; NMPFT (1937 – 3949) / Science & Society Picture Library; **W. Kilburn**, Chartists' Rally, Kennington Common, 10 April 1848, reproduced by gracious permission of Her Majesty the Queen; **A. Rosling**, The Riverfront and St. Paul's Cathedral from London Bridge, c. 1853, reproduced by gracious permission of Her Majesty the Queen; **C. de Montizon**, The Hippopotamus at the Zoological Gardens, Regent's Park, c. 1855, Royal Photographic Society (11455); **Anon**, William Smith, Aged 19, Before Deportation to Canada, c. 1856 Guildhall Library (Manuscripts Department), Corporation of London; **R. Howlett**, I. K. Brunel by the Launching Chains of the 'Great Eastern', Millwall, Isle of Dogs, November 1857, Institute of Civil Engineers; Construction of the 'Great Eastern' – side view, Millwall, Isle of Dogs, November 1857, Institute of Civil Engineers; Construction of the 'Great Eastern'– bow-on view, Millwall, Isle of Dogs, November 1857, Institute of Civil Engineers; **R. Fenton**, Westminster Abbey and the Palace of Westminster, c. 1857, Private collection; Buckingham Palace, c. 1857, Private collection; **G. Shadbolt**, Vale of Hornsey, c. 1860, Bruce Castle Museum/Haringey Museum & Archive Service; **V. Blanchard**, The River and the Palace of Westminster, c. 1860, Royal Photographic Society (3800/9); Temple Bar, Fleet Street/Strand, c. 1862, MoL (IN14862); **V. A. Prout**, Eel Pie Island, *c.* 1862, Victoria & Albert Museum (129-1987); **G. Bevington**, Bevington & Sons Tannery, Neckinger Mills, Bermondsey view of the factory from the Surrey Canal, 1862, Victoria & Albert Museum; Bevington & Sons Tannery, Neckinger Mills, Bermondsey – 'Finishing Skivers and Persians for Hat Linings and Boot Purposes', 1862, Victoria & Albert Museum; **H. Flather**, Construction of the Metropolitan District Railway, Sloane Square, c. 1866, Institute of Civil Engineers; Construction of the Metropolitan District Railway, Victoria, c. 1866, Institute of Civil Engineers; **W. Strudwick**, Statue of Richard 1, Old Palace Yard, Westminster, c. 1865, Victoria & Albert Museum (59-408); A Riverside View of Houses in Fore Street, Lambeth, c. 1866, Guildhall Library, Corporation of London (St. Pauls Collection); New Street or Princes Street, Lambeth, c. 1866, Guildhall Library, Corporation of London (St. Paul's Collection); Old Houses, Holborn Bars, c. 1868, Guildhall Library, Corporation of London (St. Paul's Collection); View Across Queen Victoria Street Towards St. Paul's Cathedral, c. 1870, Guildhall Library, Corporation of London (St. Paul's Collection); **H. Dixon**, Panorama of Holborn Viaduct Under Construction, 1869, Guildhall Library, Corporation of London (Pr.304/HOL (2)); **J. Sanford**, 'The Oxford Arms', Warwick Lane, c. 1870, Guildhall Library, Corporation of London (Norman Collection Vol. 4); **J. Hedderly**, Chelsea Riverfront from (old) Battersea Bridge, c. 1870, Guildhall Library, Corporation of London (Norman Collection Vol. 2); **Anon**, Octavious

H. Smith's Thames Bank Distillery, Grosvenor Road, SW1, c. 1870, Guildhall Library, Corporation of London (B.W2/GRO); **A. and J. Bool**, Combe & Co.'s Brewery, Castle Street, St Giles, WC2, c. 1875, MoL (IN14842); The Poor's Churchyard, St. Bartholomew's, Smithfield, 1877, MoL (IN1711); **Morgan & Laing**, General View of Canada Dock, Surrey Commercial Docks, c. 1876, MoL/Port of London Authority Collection; General View of Canada Dock, Surrey Commercial Docks, c. 1876, MoL/Port of London Authority Collection; **J. Thomson**, the 'Crawlers', c. 1877, MoL (IN648); Recruiting Sergeants, Westminster, c. 1877, MoL (IN621); Hookey Alf, c. 1877, MoL (IN647); Workers on the Silent Highway, c. 1877, MoL (IN641); 'Covent Garden Labourers', c. 1877, MoL (IN636); **H. Dixon**, St. Mary Overy's Dock, Southwark, 1881, MoL (IN1750); Shambles in Aldgate, 1883, MoL (IN1770); Shop in Macclesfield Street, Soho, 1883, MoL (IN1777); **B. Lemere**, Island Lead Mills, Limehouse, 1885, RCHME Crown Copyright (5594); **Anon for the London Stereoscopic Company**, Regent's Quadrant, c. 1886, MoL (IN4090); **F. G. O. Stuart**, Trafalgar Square, c. 1885, MoL (IN4651); **C. A. Wilson**, Piccadilly Circus, c. 1890, MoL (IN4633); Farringdon Street, Looking Towards Holborn Viaduct, c. 1890, MoL (IN4111); The Great Wheel, Earl's Court Exhibition, c. 1890, MoL (IN491); Thames at Richmond, c. 1890, MoL (IN4968); **F. P. Cembrano**, Pleasure Boats on the Thames, c. 1891, Royal Photographic Society (3281); **P. Martin**, Street Urchins, Lambeth, 1893, Victoria & Albert Museum (2889-1937); Dancing to the Organ, Lambeth, 1893, Victoria & Albert Museum (2877-1937); Blind Beggar, Caledonian Cattle Market, 1893–1894; The Old Empire Theatre, Leicester Square, 1895, Victoria & Albert Museum (2880-1937); Magazine Seller, Ludgate Circus, 1893, Victoria & Albert Museum (2900-1937); Snow on the Embankment, 1896, Victoria & Albert Museum (1686-1980); **A. J. Ransome**, The Frozen River, 1895, Royal Photographic Society (5042); **Anon for Underwood and Underwood**, Queen Victoria Driving Down Kensington Terrace, 25 June 1897, MoL (IN14855); **Rev. J. Galt**, Backyards, Spitalfields, c. 1900, MoL (IN488); Making Shovels Out of Scrap Metal – a Home Industry, Bethnal Green, c. 1900, MoL (IN434); Railway Track Maintenance Gang, Outside St. Pancras Station, c. 1900, MoL (IN483), Cat's Meat Man in an East End Street, c. 1902, MoL (IN432); **G. Davison**, Panorama of Traffic at a Busy Road Intersection, c. 1900, NMPFT/Science & Society Picture Library; **Anon for the City of Westminster Council Department of Public Works**, Collecting Street Sweepings, 1903, MoL (IN6655); Repairing a Rock Asphalt Roadway, 1903, MoL (IN6658); **Anon for the Surrey Commercial Docks Engineer's Department**, Warehousemen Loading Cheese onto a Special Loader, Canadian Produce, Warehouse West, 1906, MoL/Port of London Authority Collection; **J. H. Avery**, Drill With Barbells, Hugh Myddleton School, 1907, Greater London Photograph Library; Panorama of the Site for County Hall, 1909, Greater London Photograph Library; Catherine Court, Trinity Square, 1913, MoL/Port of London Authority Collection; Excavating Machine, Royal Albert Dock Extension South, 11 September 1913, MoL/Port of London Authority Collection; **A. L. Coburn**, Ludgate Hill, c. 1909, MoL

(IN16000); Hyde Park Corner, c. 1909, MoL; Wapping, c. 1909, MoL; St. Paul's from the River, c. 1909, MoL; Regent's Canal, Camden Lock, c. 1909, MoL; **Campbell-Gray**, Billingsgate Pier, 1907, MoL (IN14853); A Glass Lens Manufacturing Workshop, c. 1910, MoL (IN3288); **C. Broom**, Miss Christabel Pankhurst at a Suffragette Fair, May 1909, MoL (IN1334); Suffragette Demonstration, May 1909, MoL (IN1279); **W. Whiffin**, Children Following a Water Cart, c. 1910, Tower Hamlets Local History Library (Wh.682); **H. W. Nicholls**, Ludgate Circus, c. 1910, Royal Photographic Society (5493); Derby Day, Epsom, 1912 or 1914, courtesy of John Benton-Harris; **J. Sinclair**, The Haymarket in Winter, c. 1913, Royal Photographic Society (4597); **N. Smyth**, An Alley in Bromley, 1914, International Institute of Social History, Amsterdam (A32/669); A Child on a Bed in a House in Bow, 1915, International Institute for Social History, Amsterdam (A32/668); **Miles & Kay**, Addle Street from Wood Street, City of London, 8 September 1915, Guildhall Library, Corporation of London (First World War Collection); Liverpool Street, City of London, 8 September 1915, Guildhall Library, Corporation of London (First World War Collection); **F. J. Mortimer**, Soldiers Leaving for the First World War, c. 1915, Royal Photographic Society (7551); **J. H. Avery**, Quayside Crane in the Royal Victoria Dock Damaged in the Silvertown Explosion, 2 February 1917, MoL/Port of London Authority Collection; Damage Caused to Grain Silos in the Royal Victoria Dock by the Silvertown Explosion, 25 January, 1917, MoL/Port of London Authority Collection; **H. W. Nicholls**, Wounded Soldier and Woman Flag-Seller, 1918, Royal Photographic Society (4719); Women Spraying Tar, 1918, Royal Photographic Society (7359); Armistice Day Celebrations, Trafalgar Square, 1918, Royal Photographic Society (23047); **F. Judge**, So This is London, 1923, Royal Photographic Society (1607); Held Up in Trafalgar Square, 1923, Royal Photographic Society (1611); **J. Jarché**, Boys Caught Bathing in the Serpentine, 1924, Royal Photographic Society (7145); **C. Job**, Richmond Bridge, 1925, Royal Photographic Society (5314); Below London Bridge, 1936, Royal Photographic Society (7171); **W. Whiffin**, Strikers Picketing a Van in Cotton Street, Poplar, During the General Strike, May 1926, Tower Hamlets Local History Library (Wh.1104); Manchester Road, Isle of Dogs, c. 1928, Tower Hamlets Local History Library (Wh.233); **J. Dixon-Scott**, The River at Gravesend, c. 1930, MoL/Port of London Authority Collection; **G. D. Reid**, The Cobbled Causeway Under Southwark Bridge, c. 1930, MoL (IN9462); Tower of London, c. 1930, MoL (IN9528); Trafalgar Square, c. 1930, MoL (IN9125); Southwark Corporation's Rubbish Depot, Greenmoor Wharf, Bankside, c. 1930, MoL (IN9442); Buckingham Palace Floodlit, c. 1930, MoL (IN9071); Bow Lane, c. 1930, MoL (IN9394); Piccadilly Circus, c. 1930, MoL (IN9084); **H. Casparious**, Pleasure Boats, 1930, MoL (IN7844); **E. O. Hoppé**, A London Policeman, c. 1930, Mansell Collection; Bird's-eye View of the Northern Approach to London Bridge, Looking South, c. 1930, Mansell Collection, 'Billy-cock' Hat Maker, c. 1930, Mansell Collection; **Anon**, Shoppers in Sutton High Street, c.

1930, MoL; **Anon for Fox Photos**, Unemployed Girls Queuing for Work in Farringdon Street, March 1931, MoL (IN7860); Children Playing Cricket in Alpha Road, Millwall, 1938, MoL (IN4096); **H. Spender**, A Woman Leaving a Pub with a Gramophone, Whitechapel, c. 1938, MoL (IN7286); Family Group at Home, Stepney, c. 1934, MoL (IN7285); **F. H. Man**, A Pub in the Edgware Road, 1938, Piccadilly Circus, 1934; An East End Street, 1936, all courtesy of Lieselott Man; **H. A. Murch**, Busy Thames, n.d. Royal Photographic Society (6638); Nightfall at Westminster, n.d., Royal Photographic Society (6641); **A. H. Blake**, An Evening Train Leaving Cannon Street, n.d., Royal Photographic Society (538); **W. Suschitzky**, Two Men in a Café, Charing Cross Road, c. 1935, MoL (IN15420); Milk Cart, Charing Cross Road, c. 1935, MoL (IN15411); Victoria Bus Station, 1939, MoL (IN15415); Fog in the Charing Cross Road, c. 1935, MoL (IN15413); **M. Monck**, Goods Way, Near Kings Cross, c. 1935, MoL (IN15204); Woman with a Camera, Portland Town, c. 1935, MoL (IN14983); Italian Seller of Windmill Saffron Hill, c. 1935, MoL (IN15129)/Mary Evans Picture Library; **C. Arapoff**, Carpet Stall, Caledonian Market, 1935, MoL (IN14290); East End Girl, c. 1935, MoL (IN14624); Mr Mix with his Children, Hanbury Buildings, Poplar, 1939, MoL (IN14508); St. Martin's Church from the National Gallery, c. 1935, MoL (IN14349); Wapping, c. 1935, MoL (IN14289); Thames at Kew Bridge, c. 1935, MoL (IN14614); **B. Brandt**, Workman's Café, c. 1936, MoL (IN2238); Parlourmaid and Underparlourmaid Ready to Serve Dinner, c. 1936; A 'Bobby' on Point Duty, c. 1936, After the Theatre, or By No Means The Last Days of an Old Taxi, Lower Regent Street, c. 1936; all photographs courtesy of J-P Kernot; **H. Cartier-Bresson**, Coronation of George VI, 1937, Magnum Photos; **N. Griggs**, Battersea Power Station, c. 1937, Royal Photographic Society; **A. Kersting**, The Embankment and Cleopatra's Needle from Hungerford Bridge, c. 1937, MoL (IN4772), © Anthony Kersting; **H. Mason**, St Paul's Cathedral During the Blitz, 29 December 1940, MoL; **B. Brandt**, East End Underground Station Shelter, 12 November 1940, MoL (IN8719); South East London Underground Station Shelter, 11 November 1940, MoL (IN8704); South East London Underground Station Shelter, 11 November 1940, MoL (IN8727), all photographs courtesy of J-P Kernot; **A. Cross and F. Tibbs**, Queen Street Place Looking South Towards Southwark Bridge, 11 May 1941, MoL (IN7023), Lower Thames Street, 29 December 1940, MoL (IN6912); City Temple, Holborn Viaduct, 17 April 1941, MoL (IN6942); Moorgate Station, 29 December 1940, MoL (IN6845); Corn Exchange, 42 Mark Lane, 17 April 1941, MoL (IN6941); all photographs reproduced by permission of the Commissioner of Police for the City of London; **Anon for Fox Photos**, A Policeman Inspecting Bomb Damage, 1940 or 1941, The Hulton-Deutsch Collection; **Anon for Keystone Press**, Police Officers Attending to an Injured Man, 20 October 1940, The Hulton-Deutsch Collection; **G. Rodger**, Blind Beggar, Hyde Park Corner, 1940, Magnum Photos; Two Boys with a Steel Helmet, 1940, Magnum Photos; **Anon for Topical Press**, Home on Leave from BEF, Soldier Says

Goodbye to his Baby Son, 13 June 1940; Evacuation of London School Children, Soldier Saying Goodbye to his Son, 13 June 1940, all The Hulton-Deutsch Collection; **B. Hardy**, Children Running After the Parson, 23 November 1940, Man with an Injured Leg, 18 January 1941; Firefighter, 11 January 1941, all The Hulton-Deutsch Collection; **R. Speller for Fox Photos**, The Southern Railway Home Guard Receiving Tommy Gun Instruction, 11 March 1942, The Hulton-Deutsch Collection; **Anon**, Bombed Houses, 1943, Royal Photographic Society; **Anon for Keystone Press**, VE Day Celebrations, Piccadilly Circus, 8 May 1945, The Hulton-Deutsch Collection; **T. Hopkins**, Gypsy Horse Dealers, Elephant and Castle, 1948, MoL (IN15925); North London Wedding Party, 1958, MoL (IN15950), all © Thurston Hopkins; **B. Hardy**, Couple in a Room, Elephant and Castle, 1949, The Hulton-Deutsch Collection; 'Eddie', the Shoe-Black, Piccadilly, c. 1952, The Hulton-Deutsch Collection; You're Never Alone with a Strand, Albert Bridge, 1959, The Hulton-Deutsch Collection, all © Bert Hardy; **J. H. Stone**, Pool of London, c. 1948, MoL (IN15544), © John H. Stone; **N. Henderson**, Group Outside a Pub in Hammersmith on Boat Race Day, c. 1952, MoL (IN7526), **H. Grant**, Street Entertainer, c. 1950, MoL/Henry Grant Collection; Striking Dock Workers, 1951, MoL/Henry Grant Collection (1309 /24); Striking Dock Workers, 1951, MoL/Henry Grant Collection (1309/41); Youths Looking in a Clothes Shop Window, c. 1950, MoL/Henry Grant Collection (1301/5), all © MoL/Henry Grant; **M. Harker**, St. Paul's Cathedral from Cheapside, 1952, © Margaret Harker; **W. Whiffin**, Hilary House, Teviot Street, Bromley, Under Construction, c. 1953; Tower Hamlets Local History Library (Wh.1443), **I. Bidermanas**, Man Blowing Bubbles, Petticoat Lane, c. 1953; Tired Sailor, Piccadilly Circus, c. 1953, all © the Estate of Izis Bidermanas; **H. Cartier-Bresson**, London Suburbs, 1954, Magnum Photos; Newspaper Seller and City Businessman, c. 1955, Magnum Photos, all © Henri Cartier-Bresson; **R. Mayne**, Gambling Group, Southam Street, North Kensington, 1958, MoL (IN15269); Off the Harrow Road, Paddington, 1955, MoL (IN15278); Boy Trying to Catch a Football, Brindley Road, Paddington, 1956, MoL (IN15275); all © Roger Mayne; **E. Smith**, Soldiers Marching, St. James's Palace, c. 1960, MoL (IN7690); London Bridge from Fishmongers Hall, c. 1957, MoL (IN7658); A House in St. John's Wood, c. 1955, MoL (IN7743); Mending a Car and Motor Scooter, Alton Estate, Roehampton, c. 1955, MoL (IN7748), Bankside, c. 1960, MoL (IN7639); **B. Collins**, Rush Hour at Victoria Station, c.1960, MoL (IN15976), © Bob Collins; **C.T. Gifford**, Inside Old Oak Common Round-house, 26 April 1962, MoL (IN15893); Entrance to St. Pancras Station, c. 1965, MoL (IN15894), all © Colin T. Gifford; **J. Goldblatt**, Houses of Parliament, 1964; Father and Son Raising Sprouts, 1966, all © John Goldblatt; **D. Hurn**, A Stripper's Dressing Room, Soho, 1965, Magnum Photos, © David Hurn; **J. Liebling**, Youths in Enfield Park, 1967, MoL (IN15560); Outside Claridge's Hotel, 1967, MoL (IN15553), all © Jerome Liebling; **T. Ray-Jones**, Wimbledon, 1968, John Benton Harris NMPFT/

Science & Society Picture Library; **T. Spencer**, A Gang of Skinheads Passing a Group of Hippies, Piccadilly Circus, 1969, MoL (IN7444); Gang of 'Mod' Youths, Borehamwood, 1969, MoL (IN7434), all © Terry Spencer; **J. Gay**, Liverpool St. Station, c. 1972; From Blackfriars Railway Bridge Looking Towards Southwark Bridge, c. 1972, all © John Gay; **R. Perry**, 'Teds' Outside the 'Black Raven' Pub, Bishopsgate, City of London, c. 1972, MoL (IN7798); The 'Rolling Stones' in Concert, Earl's Court, c. 1976, MoL (IN7807), all © Roger Perry; **D. McCullin**, Near Spitalfields Market, 1973, Magnum Photos, © Don McCullin; **F. Mayer**, Eros at Night, 1974, Magnum Photos, © Fred Mayer; **P. Trevor**, Kids Playing, Fournier Street, E1, 1974, MoL (IN16030); Lolesworth Close, Commercial Street, E1, 1978, MoL (IN16039); Textile Sweatshop, Fournier Street, E1, 1979, MoL (IN16042), Boy with Toy Gun, Brick Lane, E1, 1978, MoL (IN16029); Girl in the Rain, Chilton Street, E2, 1977, MoL (IN16026); all © Paul Trevor; **J. Benton-Harris**, Derby Day, 1976; Charing Cross Road, 1974; The Wedding of Prince Charles and Lady Diana Spencer, 1981, all © John Benton-Harris; **I. Berry**, Doctor's Waiting Room, Battersea, c. 1975, Magnum Photos; Man Eating in the Street, Spitalfields, c. 1975, Magnum Photos; Hyde Park, c. 1975, Magnum Photos; Couple Kissing, New Year's Eve, Trafalgar Square, c. 1975, Magnum Photos; all © Ian Berry; **S. Fear**, Chinese New Year Celebrations, Gerrard Street, Soho, 1976, MoL (IN15802), © Sally Fear; **B. Lewis**, Charing Cross Station, 5.30pm, 1978, MoL (IN8208), © Barry Lewis; **J. Rice**, Couple on a Bench, Tower of London, 1979, MoL (IN7168); TV Crew at a National Front Rally, Walworth, 1980, MoL (IN7161); Van Driver, Deptford Creek, c. 1993; Eddie Stabling his Horse, Stowage, Deptford Creek, c. 1993, all © Jim Rice; **T. Evans**, King George V Dock, 1979, MoL (IN7853); Wood Street, City of London, 1990; MoL (IN15534), all © Tom Evans; **P. Barkshire**, Hay's Wharf, 1985, Whitechapel Road, 1981, MoL (IN14188); Workshop, Meard Street, Soho, 17 March 1981, MoL (IN8340); © Paul Barkshire; **P. Marlow**, Footbridge and Warehouse, Millwall Dock, 1982, Magnum Photos, © Peter Marlow; **J. R. J. Taylor**, North London Suburbia, 1982, MoL (IN15562), © John R. J Taylor; **G. Socki**, Bexleyheath, 1985, MoL (IN15682), © Garanth Socki; **Y. Matze**, Black Funeral, Kensal Green Cemetery, c. 1985, MoL (IN14805), Kensal Green Cemetery, Harrow Road, W10, c. 1985, MoL (IN14802); all © Yoke Matze; **C. Wroblewski**, South London Skinhead, c. 1985, MoL (IN15727), © Chris Wroblewski; **B. Tapper**, Whitechapel High Street, 1986, MoL (IN15749), © Bob Tapper; **J. Friedman**, Panorama of Piccadilly Circus, 1988, MoL (IN15574) © Jim Friedman; **A. Fox**, Female Office Worker, 1987, MoL (IN15577); Salesmen in a City Pub, 1987, MoL (IN15578), commissioned by MoL and Camerawork, © Anna Fox; **A. Delaney**, Martello Street, London Fields, E8, 1989, MoL (IN15860); Annett's Crescent, Essex Road, N1, 1989, MoL (IN15858); Canary Wharf, Isle of Dogs, 1991, MoL (IN15857), all © Alan Delaney; **T. Daly**, Fleet Street, 1988, MoL (IN15691) from 'The Monopoly Board', exhibited at The Photographers' Gallery, London 1988–1989, © Tim Daly; **A. Cook**, Looking North from Philpot Lane, City of London, 11.57pm, c. 1990, © Andy Cook; **C. Dorley-Brown**, X-ray Patient, Homerton Hospital, Hackney, 1988, MoL (IN15631), © Chris Dorley-Brown; **E. Barber**, Bill and Dolly Luff, Loraine Estate, Holloway, c. 1989, MoL (IN15484), © Ed Barber; **M. Segal**, Single Mother with her Children, Camberwell, SE5, 1991, MoL (IN16017); Lubavitch Hassidic Family, Stamford Hill, 1993, MoL (IN16016), all © Magda Segal; **K. Cardwell**, Sunday Market, Cheshire Street, E2, 1991, MoL, © Keith Cardwell; **P. Baldesare**, Early Morning Commuter, London, Metropolitan Line, © Paul Baldesare; **M. Seaborne**, 'The Best Future for Britain' – Demolition of Deptford Power Station, April 1992, MoL; Docklands Light Railway, Limeharbour, September 1987, MoL, all © Mike Seaborne; **D. Trainer**, Beggar, Oxford Circus Underground Station, 1994; Travellers, Epsom Fair, June 1994, all © David Trainer; **P. Marshall**, Carter Lane, EC4, 1992; Panoramic View of the Docklands Light Railway Beckton Extension Under Construction, 1992, all © Peter Marshall; **T. Hunter and J. Mackinnon**, London Fields – The Ghetto, 1994, MoL, © Tom Hunter and James Mackinnon.

SELECT BIBLIOGRAPHY

St. John Adcock (ed), *Wonderful London*, The Educational Book Co. Ltd, London, n.d.

Diane Atkinson (ed), *Mrs Broom's Suffragette Photographs*, Dirk Nishen Publishing, London, 1988

Ed Barber, *Islington's People*, Islington Council Press, London, n.d.

Paul Barkshire, *Unexplored London*, Leonard Publishing, Wheathampstead, 1987

Paul Barkshire, *Other London*, Leonard Publishing, Wheathampstead, 1989

Hilaire Belloc (ed), *London*, with photographs by Alvin Langdon Coburn, London, 1909

Ian Berry, *The English*, Allen Lane/Penguin Books, London, 1978

John Betjeman and John Gay, *London's Historic Railway Stations*, John Murray, London, 1972

Izis Bidermanas, *Gala Day in London*, Harvill Press, London, 1953

Bill Brandt, *The English at Home*, Batsford, London, 1936

Bill Brandt, *A Night in London*, Batsford, London, 1938

Bill Brandt, *Camera in London*, Focal Press, London and New York, 1948

Bill Brandt, *Shadow of Light,* Gordon Fraser, London, 1977

Bill Brandt, *London in the Thirties*, Gordon Fraser, London, 1983

Bill Brandt, *The Golden Summer: The Edwardian Photographs of Horace W. Nicholls*, Pavilion Books, London, 1989

Graham Bush (ed), *Old London*, with photographs by Henry Dixon, Alfred & John Bool, and William Strudwick, Academy Editions, London and New York, 1975

Robert Cowan (ed), *London After Dark*, with photographs by Alan Delaney, Phaidon Press, London, 1993

Richard Ehrlich (ed), *Tony Ray-Jones*, Cornerhouse Publications, Manchester, 1990

Chris Ellmers (ed), *George Reid: River Thames*, Dirk Nishen Publishing, London, 1987

Roy Flukinger, Larry Schaaf and Standish Meacham (eds), *Paul Martin: Victorian Photographer*, Gordon Fraser, London, 1978

Anna Fox, *Workstations*, Camerawork, London, 1988

Helmut Gernsheim, *The History of Photography*, Oxford University Press, London, New York and Toronto, 1955

Colin T. Gifford, *Decline of Steam*, Ian Allen Ltd, London, 1965

Colin T. Gifford, *Each a Glimpse*, Ian Allen Ltd, London, 1970

Bert Hardy, *My Life*, Gordon Fraser, London, 1985

Charles Harvard (ed), *Victorian Snapshots*, with photographs by Paul Martin, Country Life Ltd, London, 1939

Mark Haworth-Booth (ed), *The Street Photographs of Roger Mayne*, The Victoria & Albert Museum, London, 1986

294

Tom Hopkinson (ed), *Bert Hardy*, Gordon Fraser in association with The Arts Council of Great Britain, London, 1975

E. O. Hoppé, *London*, The Medici Society, London, 1932, and B. Arthaud, Grenoble, 1932

E. O. Hoppé, *The Image of London*, Chatto & Windus, London, 1936

E. O. Hoppé, *A Camera on Unknown London*, J.M.Dent and Sons, London, 1936

E. O. Hoppé, *The London of George VI*, J.M.Dent and Sons, London, 1937

Ian Leith, *The Streets of London, Vol. 1: Westminster Photographed by Bedford Lemere*, Editions, Liverpool, 1990

Felix Man, *Man with Camera: Photographs from Seven Decades*, Secker and Warburg, London, 1983

Michael Pritchard, *A Directory of London Photographers 1841–1908*, ALLM Books, Watford, 1986

Tony Ray-Jones, *A Day Off: an English Journal*, Thames & Hudson, London, 1974

Jim Rice, *Deptford Creek*, Cornerhouse Publications, Manchester, and the Museum of London, London, 1993

Raphael Samuel (ed), *Wolf Suschitzky: Charing Cross Road in the Thirties,* Dirk Nishen Publishing, London, 1988

Mike Seaborne (ed), *George Reid: Streets of London,* Dirk Nishen Publishing, London, 1987

Mike Seaborne (ed), *Arthur Cross and Fred Tibbs: The London Blitz*, Dirk Nishen Publishing, London, 1987

Mike Seaborne (ed), *Cyril Arapoff: London in the Thirties*, Dirk Nishen Publishing, London, 1988

Magda Segal, *London at Home,* Cornerhouse Publications, Manchester, 1994

Adolphe Smith and John Thomson, *Street Life in London*, Sampson Low, Marston, Searle and Rivington, London, 1877–1878

Edwin Smith, *The Living City*, Corporation of London, London, 1957, (new ed.1966)

John R. J. Taylor, *Ideal Home*, Cornerhouse Publications, Manchester, 1989

Roger Taylor, *George Washington Wilson: Artist and Photographer 1823–93*, Aberdeen University Press, Aberdeen, 1981

Stephen White (ed), *John Thomson, Life and Photographs*, Thames & Hudson, London, 1985

Val Williams, *Women Photographers*, Virago, London, 1986

Chris Wroblewski and Nelly Gommez-Vaez, *City Indians*, Eichborn Verlag, Frankfurt, 1983

INDEX

Numbers appearing in **bold** indicate photographs, with or without text.

A

Addle Street 1915	108
advertising photography	
Strand cigarettes	**193**
Albert Bridge 1959	**193**
albumen prints	**39, 42–3, 47–57,**
	60–2, 65–6, 73–5, 83
gold toned	76, 77–8
Aldgate 1883	**71**
Alpha Road 1938	**137**
Alton Estate c. 1955	**213**
Amateur Photographer and	
Photographic News	112
American photographers	9, 27
Benton-Harris, John	9, 27,
	238–41
Coburn, Alvin Langdon	21,
	95–7, bib 294
Liebling, Jerome	27, 199, **221–2**
Annett's Crescent 1989	**268**
Arapoff, Cyril	9, **150–5**
architectural photographers	36, 52,
	56, 63, 73, 75, 92, 163, 200,
	210, 228, 260, 267, 271
architectural photography	11, 17,
	44–5, 52–5, 63–4, 71–2, 74,
	93, 126–9, 153, 162,
	200–1, 211–3,
	228, 252–5, 267–9, 271
Arthur Cross and Fred Tibbs:	
The London Blitz	bib 295
Arts Council	29, 242, 247
Astor, John Jacob, 1st Baron,	
c. 1912	103–**4**
Austrian photographers	
Suschitzky, W.	9, **144–6**, bib 295
Autotype Company	81
Avery, John H.	21, **92–4**, 110–11

B

Baldesare, Paul	277
Bankside c. 1960	**214**
Barber, Ed	9, **273**, bib 294
barges *see* ships	
Barkshire, Paul	9, **254–6**, bib 294
Battersea interior c. 1975	**242**
Battersea Power Station	
c. 1937	**162**
Beard, Richard	8, 19
beggars c. 1893	80–**81**
1940	**176**
1994	**280**
see also poverty	
Benington, Walter	21
Benton-Harris, John	9, 27, **238–41**
Bermondsey 1862	**49**
Berry, Ian	9, 29, **242–5**, bib 294
Bert Hardy	bib 294
Bethnal Green c. 1900	**87**
Betjeman, Sir John	228, bib 294
Bevington, Geoffrey	**49**
Bexleyheath 1985	**259**
Bidermanas, Iziz	27, **202–4,**
	bib 294
Big Ben *see* Palace of Westminster	
Billingsgate Pier 1907	**98**
Bishopsgate c. 1972	**230**
Blackfriars railway bridge	
c. 1972	**229**
Blake, A. H. 'Cockney'	112, **143**
Blanchard, Valentine	17, **47**
bomb damage	25
First World War	**108–9**
Second World War	**166,**
	170–5, 184
IRA	**271**
see also explosion damage	
Bool, Alfred and John	19, 56,
	60, **63–4**, bib 294
Borehamwood 1969	224–**225**
Bow house interior 1915	106–**107**

Bow Lane c. 1930 **128**

Brandt, Bill 10, 23, 25, 150, 156,
157–60, **167–9**, bib 294

breweries **62–3**

Brick Lane area 29, **234–7**

bridges 21

Blackfriars railway bridge
c. 1972 **229**

DLR crossing, River Lea
1992 283

Hungerford Suspension Bridge
1845 **36–37**

London Bridge c. 1930 **132**

c. 1957 **211**

railway bridge, Ludgate
c. 1909 **95**

Richmond 1925 **120**

Southwark

c. 1930 125

1941 **170**

c. 1972 **229**

Brindley Road 1956 209

British Journal of Photography 46

British Museum 44

Bromley c. 1953 **201**

Bromley-by-Bow 1914 **106**

bromoil prints **112**, **162**

bromoil transfer prints **118**

Broom, Christina **100–1**

Brunel, Isambard Kingdom 17

grave site 261

Great Eastern steamship **42–3**

Hungerford Suspension Bridge
36, **37**

Buckingham Palace c. 1857 44, **45**

c. 1930 **126**

buildings *see* architectural
photography; engineering works;
high-rise buidings; historic
buildings; housing; hospitals;
hotels; industrial
photography

burial ceremonies **260**

C

café life c. 1935 **144**

c. 1936 156, **157**

Caledonian Market

c. 1893 80, **81**

1935 **150**

calotypes 17, **37**, 39, 44

Camberwell family 1991 **274**

Camden Lock c. 1909 **97**

Camera in London bib 294

Camera on Unknown
London bib 295

camera techniques

differential focusing **136**

narrow depth of field **175**

ultra-wide angle lens **276**

see also candid photography

cameras 17

Contax 23, 139

'Facile' detective cameras 19,
80, 81

hand-held 19, 23, 105

Kodak 19, **89**

large-format 11, 92, 111, 175,
185, 254, 284

Leica 23, 140

miniature 140, 150

night photography 118, 140

roll-film 23, 150

Rollieflex 23, 150

swing-lens panoramic 19, **89**
264–5, **282–3**

without viewfinder 125

Camerawork Gallery 29, 234, 266

Campbell-Gray **98–9**

Canada Dock c. 1876 **65**

Canary Wharf 1991 **269**

candid photography 11, 19, **47**, 76,
77, **80–1**, 140, **141**,
147, 207, 249

see also street life

Cannon Street

train departing (n.d.) **143**

carbon printing 52, 56

carbon prints **63–4**, **70–2**, **82**,
120–1, **143**

Cardwell, Keith **276**

Carter Lane 1992 **282**

Cartier-Bresson, Henri 23, 27,
161, **205–6**, 207, 258

Casparious, Hans **130**

Castle Street c. 1875 **63**

Ce Soir 161

celebrations

Armistice Day 1918 **115**

Chinese New Year 1976 **246**

Coronation of George VI
1937 161

Diamond Jubilee 1897 83

New Year's Eve 1975 242, **245**

Royal Wedding 1981 **240–1**

VE Day 1945 185

see also recreation

Cembrano, F.P. **79**

cemeteries **260–1**

censorship, wartime 25, 27,
180–81

Charing Cross Road

c. 1935 **144–6**

1974 **239**

Charing Cross Road in the
Thirties 144, bib 295

Charing Cross Station 1978 **247**

Chartist Rally 1848 **38**

Chelsea 61

riverfront c. 1870 61

Cheshire Street 1991 **276**

Cheyne Walk 1870s 61

children **68**, **80**, **92**, **102**,
106–7, **137**, **141**, 150
151–2, 176, **177–80**,
209, **236–7**, **274**

see also families

Chilton Street 1977 **237**

Chinese New Year 1976 **246**

Church Army 98

churches

St. Albans 1990 **253**

St. Andrew-by-the-Wardrobe
c. 1870 **55**

St. Martin's c. 1935 **153**

St. Mary Aldermary
c. 1930 **128**

St. Mary Axe c. 1990 **271**

see also St. Paul's Cathedral
Westminster Abbey

Cibachrome prints **264–5**

City Indians **262**, bib 295

City of London 25, 52, **108–9**,
125, 170, 200, **206**, **211**,
230, 252–**253**, **271**

Guldhall Library 21

police *see* police photography;
policemen

City of Westminster **44–5**, **47**,
55, **68**, **90**, 125,
142, **218**, bib 295

Council 21, 90

City Temple 1941 170, **172**

Claridges' Hotel 1967 **222**

Cleopatra's Needle c. 1937 **163**

Clerkenwell c. 1910 **99**

c. 1935 147, **149**

cloud negatives **65**

Coburn, Alvin Langdon 21,
95–7, bib 294

'Cockney' *see* Blake, A.H.

collage **284–5**

collections of photography 8, 10,
21, 29

Collins, Bob **215**

colour coupler prints **259**, **263**,
266, **270**, **272**, **277–9**, **282**

colour photography 29, 130, 162

colour transparencies **184**, **233**,
240–1, **271**

Commercial Street 1974 **235**

commissioning photography 21,

29, 42, 50, 52, 56, 63–5,
90, 98, 113, 123, 124, 156,
266, 270, 273, 274
commuting **132**, **215**, **247**, **277**
construction *see* engineering
works
Contax 23, 139
Cook, Andy **271**
Corn Exchange 1941 **173**
Corporation of London 56, 211
Cotton Street 1926 **122**
County Hall, site of, 1909 **93**
Covent Garden c. 1877 **69**
Creative Camera 29
Cross, Arthur 25, **170–3**,
bib 295
Cundall, Joseph 42
*Cyril Arapoff: London in the
Thirties* bib 295

D

Daguerreotypes **34**, **38**
patenting 17, 34
daily newspapers 21, 119, 276
Daly, Tim **270**
Davison, George 19, 89
Day Off: An English Journal
bib 295
de-industrialisation *see* industrial
decline
'decisive moment' photography
161, 185, 205
Decline of Steam 216, bib 294
Delaney, Alan 30, **267–9**, bib 294
demolition works 17, 56, 147, **278**
demonstrations
Chartists' Rally 1848 **38**
dockworkers' strike
1951 196, **197–8**
General Strike pickets
1926 **122**
National Front Rally
1980 **249**

suffragettes 1909 **101**
Depression (1930s) **136**
Deptford Creek c. 1993 **250–1**
Deptford Creek 251, bib 295
digital imaging 30, 264
Directory of London
Photographers 1841–1908
bib 295
distilleries **62**
Dixon, Henry 17,19, **56–7**,
70–2, bib 294
Dixon-Scott **124**
dock workers 1951 **197–8**
Docklands 29, **252**, **254**, **269**,
Light Railway **279**, **283**
docks 91
Canada c. 1876 **65**
King George V 1979 **252**
Millwall 1982 **257**
Regent's Canal 1885 **73**
Royal Albert 1913 **94**
Royal Victoria 1917 **110–11**
1966 218–**219**
documentary photography
see social documentary
photography
Dorley-Brown, Chris **272**
Downes, George 42
Duke Street, Chelsea c. 1870 **61**
Dutch photographers
Matze, Yoke **260–1**

E

Each a Glimpse 218, bib 294
Earls Court
Exhibition c. 1890 76, **78**
Rolling Stones Concert
c. 1976 230
East End 29, **86–88**, **102**,
139–41, 149, 150, **151**, 167,
180, **181**, 195, **201**, **234–7**,
242, **243**, **255**, **263**, 276
see also Isle of Dogs

'East Thames Corridor' 259
Eastman Kodak Co. *see* Kodak
Edgware Road 1938 **140**
Eel Pie Island c. 1862 **48**
Elephant and Castle
1948 **188**
interior 1949 **190**
Embankment 1896 **81**
c. 1937 **163**
endangered buildings *see*
Society for Photographing
Relics of Old London
Enfield Park 1967 **221**
engineering works 17
Docklands Light Railway **283**
docks **65**, **94**
Holborn Viaduct **56–7**
shipbuilding (Great Eastern)
42–3
underground (Metropolitan
Line) **50–1**
English, The 242, bib 294
English at Home, The 156, 242,
bib 294
English character 27, 29,
166, 238
entertainment *see* recreation
environmental awareness 29, 30,
46, 252
Epsom
Fair 1994 **281**
race course (Derby Day)
c. 1912 103–**104**
1976 **238**
Evans, Tom 30
explosion damage **110–11**
see also bomb damage
exposure times 11,17, 34, 36, 47,
62, 81, 91, 139

F

'Facile' detective cameras 19,
80–1

factories *see* industrial
photography
families
Camberwell 1991 **274**
Poplar 1939 **152**
Royal Victoria Dock 1966
218, **219**
Stamford Hill 1993 **275**
Stepney c. 1934 **139**
see also children
Farringdon Street c. 1890 76, **77**
1931 **136**
fashion c. 1950 **199**
1969 **224–5**
tattoos **262**
Fear, Sally **246**
Fenton, Roger 17, **44–5**
firefighting 1941 180, **182**
Flather, Henry 17, **50–1**
Fleet Street c. 1862 **47–8**
1988 **270**
Fore Street 1866 **52**
Fournier Street 1974 **234**
1979 **235**
Fox, Anna **266**, bib 294
Fox Photos 21, **174**, **183**
Fox Talbot, William Henry 17, **36–7**
French photographers
Cartier-Bresson, Henri 23,
27, **161**, **205–6**, 207, 258
St. Croix, M.de 17, **34–5**
Friedman, Jim **264**

G

Gala Day London 27, 202,
bib 294
galleries 9, 29,
Camerawork 29, 234, 266
Half Moon 29, 234
Photographers' Gallery 29,
257, 270
Royal Adelaide Gallery of
Practical Science 34

Galt, Rev. John   21, **86–8**
Garai, Bert   175
Gay, John   **228–9**
gelatine dry plates   19
General Strike 1926   **122**
George Reid: River Thames
        bib 294
George Reid: Streets of London
        bib 295
George Washington Wilson:
    Artist and Photographer
        bib 295
German photographers   23
    Brandt, Bill   23, 25, 156,
        157–60, **167–9**, bib 294
    Casparious, Hans   **130**
    Hoppé, Emil Otto   21, **131–3**
    Man, Felix H.   9, 23, **140–1**
Gerrard Street 1976   **246**
Gifford, Colin T.   **216–7**, bib 294
Goldblatt, John   **218–9**
Golden Summer: Edwardian
    Photographs of Horace W.
        Nicholls   bib 294
Grant, Henry   29, **196–9**
gravure *see* photogravures
Gravesend c. 1930   **124**
'Great Eastern' (ship)   **42–3**
Griggs, Noel   **162**
Grosvenor Road c. 1870   **62**

H

Hackney 1989   **268**
    1994   **284–5**
Homerton Hospital 1988   **272**
Half Moon Gallery   29, 234
Hammersmith c. 1952   **195**
Hardy, Bert   9, 25, 27, **180–2**,
        188, **190–3**, bib 294–5
Harker, Margaret   **200**
Harrison, Tom   27
Mass Obsevation Team   138
hatmaking c. 1930   **133**

Haymarket c. 1913   **105**
health care
    a doctor's waiting room   **242**
    in a hospital   **272**
Hedderly, James   **61**
Henderson, Nigel   **195**
high-rise buildings
    commercial:
        Canary Wharf 1991   **269**
        Lloyds Building c. 1990   **271**
    domestic:
        Bromley c. 1953   **201**
        Roehampton c. 1955   **213**
high society c. 1912   **103–104**
    1930s   **156–157**
    1952   **195**
    1976   **238**
historic buildings   17, 19, **52, 54**,
        56, 63–64, 70, 71–2,102,
            126–129, 254
    see also Society for
        Photographing Relics
        of Old London
Holborn Bars c. 1868   52, **54**
Holborn Viaduct 1869   **56–7**
    c. 1890   76–**77**
    1941   **172**
Holloway c. 1989   **273**
Home Guard   **183**
Hopkins, Thurston   27, **188–9**
Hoppé, Emil Otto   21, **131–3**
        bib 295
Hornsey, Vale of, c. 1860   **46**
hospitals   **272**
hotels   **222**
Houses of Parliament *see* Palace
    of Westminster
housing
    Aldgate 1883   **71**
    backyards c. 1900   **86**
    Bethnal Green home industry
        c. 1900   **87**
        bombed 1943   **184**

Bow interior 1915   **107**
Bromley, high-rise c. 1953   **201**
Camberwell interior 1991   **274**
Commercial Street 1978   **235**
decoration 1902   **88**
Elephant and Castle interior
    1949   **190**
Fore Street slum c. 1866   **52**
Holborn Bars (16th century)
    c. 1868   52, **54**
interiors, multicultural   **274–5**
London Fields squats 1994
        284–5
Paddington 'prefabs'
    1955   **208**
Poor's Churchyard
    1877   63–**64**
Poplar tenement block
    1939   **152**
Roehampton high-rise
    c. 1955   **213**
St John's Wood
    c. 1955   **212**
squatted houses
    1994   **284–5**
Stamford Hill interior
    1993   **275**
Stepney interior
    1934   **139**
studio appartment
    conversions 1989   **267**
    suburbs 1954   **205**
Howlett, Robert   **42–3**
Hungarian photographers
    Garai, Bert   175
    Lorant, Stefan   23, 140
Hungerford Suspension Bridge
    c. 1845   **36–7**
Hunter, Tom   30, **284–5**
Hurn, David   **220**
Hyde Park c. 1975   **243**
Hyde Park Corner c. 1909   **96**
    1940   **176**

I

ICA, Independent Group   195
Ideal Home   258, bib 295
Illustrated London News   21, 42
Image of London   131, bib 295
immigrants   147, **149, 235**,
            263, 275
Imperial War Museum   113
Impressionism, influence on
    photography
    see pictorialism
industrial decline   **214, 229**,
        250–2, 255–7, 259,
            270, 278
industrial photographers
        65, 136, 162
industrial photography
    breweries   **62–3**
    distilleries   **62**
    fishing   **98**
    hatmaking   **133**
    home industry   87
    leadworks   **73**
    lens manufacture   **99**
    news and print   **270**
    power station   **162**
    railway yards   **147, 217**
    rubbish disposal   **125**
    shipbuilding   **42–3**
    tanneries   **49**
    textile sweatshop   **236**
    workshops   **99, 236, 256**
inns
    Oxford Arms c. 1870   **60**, 63
    see also public houses
Institute of Contemporary Arts
    see ICA
intaglio prints *see* photogravures;
Woodburytypes
interior photography   10
    brewery   **62**
    doctor's waiting room   **242**

homes   106–**107**, **139**, 258,
                273–5, **284–5**

hospital   **272**

warehouse   **91**

Isle of Dogs 1857   **42–3**

1885   **73**

c. 1928   122, **123**

1938   **137**

1982   **257**

1980s   **278–9**

1991   **269**

Islington Borough Council   273

Islington's People   273, bib 294

J

Jarché, James   21, **119**

Job, Charles   21, **120–1**

John Thompson: Life and
   Photographs   bib 295

Judge, Fred   **118**

K

Kennington Common 1848   **38**

Kensal Green Cemetery
   c. 1985   **260–1**

Kensington Terrace 1897   **83**

Kersting, Anthony   **163**

Keystone Press   175, **185**

Kilburn, William   **38**

King George V Dock 1979   **252**

Kings Cross, rail goods yard
   c. 1935   **147**

Kodak   8
   cameras   19, **89**

L

labourers *see* working people

Lambeth c. 1866   52, **53–4**

c. 1893   **80–81**

landscape photographers   8, 17,
    46, **48**, **79**, **124**, 131, 210,
        257, 271, 278, 282

Lea, River 1992   **283**

leadworks   **73**

Leica   23, 140

Leicester Square 1895   80–**81**

leisure *see* recreation

Lemere, Henry Bedford   **73**,
                bib 295

Lewis, Barry   29, **247**

Liebling, Jerome   27, 199, **221–2**

Life magazine   25, 27, 176, 224

Lilliput   156

Limeharbour 1987   **279**

Limehouse 1885   **73**

Linked Ring Brotherhood   89,
                112, 143

Lithuanian photographers
   Bidermanas, Izis   **202–4**

'Little Italy' *see* Saffron Hill

Liverpool Street 1915   108–**109**

Liverpool Street Station 1972   **228**

Living City, The   27, bib 295

London (1909)   95, bib 294

London (1932)   131, bib 295

London After Dark   267, bib 294

London at Home   275, bib 295

London Blitz   25, **166**, **170–77**,
                184, bib 295

London Bridge c. 1930   **132**
   c. 1957   **211**

London City Mission   21, 86

London County Council   21, 92
   County Hall site   **93**
   housing policy 1950s   213
   School of Photo-Engraving   95

London Fields 1989   **268**
   1994   30, **284–5**

London in the Thirties   bib 294

London of George VI, The
                bib 295

London Salon of Photography   112

'London Season' c. 1912   **104**
   1976   **238**

London Stereoscopic and
   Photographic Company   19, 74

London's Historic Railway
   Stations   228, bib 294

Lorant, Stefan   23, 140

Lower Thames Street 1940   **171**

Ludgate Circus 1893   **81**
   c. 1910   **103**

Ludgate Hill c. 1909   **95**

M

Macclesfield Street 1883   **72**

McCullin, Don   232

machinery
   crane, quayside   **111**
   excavating   **94**
   warehouse   **91**

Mackinnon, James   30, **284–5**

Magnum Photos   27, 29, 176,
        220, 232, 233, 242, 257

Man, Felix H.   9, 23, **140–1**,
                bib 295

Man with Camera   bib 295

Manchester Road c. 1928   **123**

markets
   Caledonian
      c. 1893–1894   **80–1**
      1935   **150**
   Covent Garden c. 1877   **69**
   Spitalfields 1973   **232**
      1991   **276**
   see also street traders

Marlow, Peter   **257**

Marshall, Peter   30, **282–3**

Martello Street 1989   **267**

Martin, Paul   19, **80–1**, 89,
                bib 294

Mason, Herbert   **166**

Matze, Yoke   **260–1**

Mayer, Fred   **233**

Mayhew, Henry   19

Mayne, Roger   27, **207–9**, 236,
                bib 294

Meard Street 1981   **256**

Metropolitan District Railway

c. 1866   **50–1**, 70

Miles & Kay   **108–9**

Millwall 1857   **42–3**
   1938   **137**

Millwall Dock 1982   **257**

modern silver prints   **86–8**,
        100–1, **104**, **106**, **130**,
        138–9, **144–7**, **149**,
        160, **174–183**, **185**,
        205–9, **215**, **221–2**, **246**
   see also silver prints

Monck, Margaret   23, **147–9**

de Montizon, Count   17, 40

Moorgate Station 1940   **172**

Morgan & Laing   **65**

Mortimer, Francis James   **112**

motor vehicles 1926   **122**
   c. 1935   **145**
   c. 1936   **160**
   c. 1955   **213**
   c. 1993   **250**
   see also traffic

moving objects photographed
        11, 34, 36, 40, **47**

multicultural London   **274–5**
   see also immigrants

multiple prints   17, 36

Murch, Horace A.   **142**

Museum of London, Historic
   Photographs Collection
                8, 10, 29,
   commissions   29, 247, 266,
                274
   curator   29, 278
   purchases   234

My Life   bib 294

N

Neckinger Mills 1862   **49**

negative types
   glass (wet collodion)   17, **40**,
                44–5
   paper (calotypes)   17, **36–7**

waxed paper   **39**
Nelson's Column 1843   36–**37**
Nicholls, Horace W.   21,
   103–104, **113**–**5**
night photography   **81**, 118,
   126, 140, **141**–**2**,
   190, **193**, **233**, **245**,
   257, **267**–9, 271
Night in London, A   bib 294
North Kensington 1958   27, **207**

O

Old London   bib 294
Old Oak Common Depot 1962
   216
Old Palace Yard Westminster
   c. 1865   **53**
Oxford Arms c. 1870   **60**, 63
Oxford Circus Underground
   Station 1994   **280**

P

Paddington 1955–6   **208**–**9**
paddle steamer 'Citizen'
   c. 1870   **61**
Palace of Westminster
   c. 1857   44–**45**
   c. 1860   **47**
   c. 1865   **53**
   (n.d.)   **142**
   1964   **218**
Pankhurst, Christabel   **100**
panoramic views   19, **56**–**7**, 89,
   93, **264**–**5**, **282**–**3**, **284**–**5**
Paul Martin: Victorian
   Photographer   bib 294
Perry, Roger   **230**–**31**
Petticoat Lane
   c. 1953   **204**
photo-reportage   23, 25, 27, 80,
   138, **140**–**41**, **150**, **156**
   see also photojournalism
Photographer's Gallery   29,

   257, 270
photographic illustration in
   publications   21, 23, 27, 29,
   95, 106, 119, 131, 138,
   140–1, 144, 150, 156,
   180, 202, 210, 215,
   223, 248, 273
Photographic Institution   42
Photographic Journal   79
photographic press agencies
   21, 25
   Fox Photos   21, **136**–**7**, **174**,
   183
   Keystone Press   **175**, **185**
   Topical Press   **178**–**9**
photographic sculpture (3-D)   30,
   284–**5**
photographic societies *see* Linked
   Ring Brotherhood, Photographic
   Society of London, Royal
   Photographic Society;
   Society for Photographing
   Relics of Old London
Photographic Society of London
   17, 39, 40, 44, 46
photographic studios   8, 9, 75, 98
photography
   as an art form   21, 67
   see also pictorialism
   beginnings of   8, 17
   collections *see* collections of
   photography
   commissioning *see*
   commissioning
   education   29, 95, 200, 220,
   223, 238
   market for   17, 19, 47, 52, 83
   trends in   11, 30, 153, 264
Photography   9
photogravures   **95**–**7**, **105**
photojournalism   9, 27, 29, 80,
   112, 176, 180, 188, 190,
   202, 215, 224, 232, 233,

   242, 246, 257
Piccadilly Circus c. 1890   76, **77**
   c. 1930   **129**
   1934   140, **141**
   1945   **185**
   c. 1952   190, **192**
   1953   202, **203**
   1969   **224**
   Eros at night 1974   **233**
   panorama 1988   **264**–**5**
pictorialism   21, 89, **95**–**7**, **105**,
   118, **120**–**1**, **142**
   modern pictorialism   **264**–**5**
Picture Post   9, 23, 25, 27,
   138, 140, 152, 156,
   180, 188–190
pigment processes, bromoil and
   oil   105
   see also bromoil prints
platinum prints   **82**, **89**
police photography   25, **38**,
   170–**173**
policemen c. 1930   **131**
   c. 1936   156, **158**
   1940   **174**–**5**
Polytechnic of Central London,
   School of Photography   **200**
Pool of London 1936   **121**
Poplar c. 1910   **102**
   1926   **122**
   interior, tenement 1939   **152**
Port of London Authority   21, 91,
   92, **94**, 98,
   110–**11**, 123, **124**
Portland Town c. 1935   **147**–**8**
portrait photographers   8, 21, 38,
   47, 63, 98, 131, 150, 274
portraits   8, 9, 10, 17
   beggars c. 1893   80, **81**
   1940   **176**
   1994   **280**
   commuter 1994   **277**
   couple kissing

   c. 1975   **245**
   couple on a bench 1979   **248**
   'Crawlers of St Giles'
   c. 1877   **67**
   hippo c. 1855   **40**
   homeless youth c. 1856   **41**
   Pankhurst, Christabel
   1909   **100**
   policemen c. 1930   **131**
   c. 1936   156, **158**
   1940   **174**–**5**
   sailor c. 1953   **203**
   shoppers c. 1930   **134**–**5**
   soldier, wounded, 1918   **113**
   squatters 1994   **284**–**5**
   see also children; families;
   recreation; street traders;
   working people; youth
postcards   100, 118
poverty   41, **67**, 86, 140, **141**,
   188, **190**, **232**, **244**
   see also beggars
power stations
   Battersea c. 1937   **162**
   Deptford 1992   **278**
press photographers   21, 25,
   100, 119, 166, 183
   see also photographic press
   agencies; photojournalism
Princes Skating Rink,
   Knightsbridge 1909   **100**
processing and printing firms
   8–9, 17
propaganda photography
   wartime   25, **174**–**5**, **178**–**9**
Prout, Victor Albert   **48**
public houses
   c. 1877, outside the Mitre and
   Dove, Westminster   **68**
   c. 1930 Olde Watling Tavern,
   Bow Lane   **128**
   c. 1938 Whitechapel   **138**
   1938 Edgware Road   **140**

c. 1952 outside a Hammersmith
pub **195**
c. 1972 Black Raven,
Bishopsgate **230**
1987 inside a City pub **266**

Q

Queen Street Place 1941 **170**
Queen Victoria Street c. 1870 **55**

R

racism 234, **231**, **249**
railways 17, 216–7
bridges 1909 **95**
c. 1972 **229**
goods yard near Kings Cross
147
maintenance depot 1962 **216**
stations **112**, 228
Cannon Street (n.d.) **143**
Charing Cross 1978 **247**
Liverpool Street c. 1972 **228**
Moorgate 1940 **172**
St Pancras c. 1900 86, **87**
c. 1965 **217**
Victoria c. 1960 **215**
Ransome, A.J. **82**
Ray-Jones, Tony 9, 27, **223**,
bib 294, 295
recreation
c. 1890, Great Wheel, Earls
Court 76, **78**
1891 pleasure boats on the
Thames **79**
1893 dancing to the organ
80, **81**
c. 1912 Derby Day 103, **104**
1924 bathing in the Serpentine
119
1930 pleasure boats on the
Thames **130**
c. 1935 woman with camera
147, **148**

1936 night life **160**
1938 cricket in the street **137**
c. 1938, gramaphone, public
house **138**
c. 1950 street entertainer **196**
1952 Boat Race Day **195**
1953 bubble blowing **204**
1958 gambling group **207**
c. 1976 Rolling Stones concert
230–31
1976 Derby Day **238**
1993 horse stabling **251**
1990s football supporters 280
see also celebrations
redevelopment works 17, 29,
201, 234, **235**, 252, **253–4**,
267–69, **269**, **278–9**
Regent Street 1936 **160**
Regent's Canal c. 1935 **147**
1930s **155**
Camden Lock c. 1909 **97**
Dock 1885 **73**
Regent's Park Zoological Gardens
c. 1855 **40**
Regent's Quadrant c. 1886 **74**
Reid, George Davison 21,
125–129, bib 294, 295
reversed images
(direct positive) **34**
Rice, Jim
9, 29, **248–51**, bib 295
Richmond c. 1890 76, **78**
Richmond Bridge 1925 **120**
roads 17
repairing 1903 **90**
1918 **114**
sweeping 1903 **90**
traffic at intersection
c. 1900 **89**
Rodger, George 25, **176–7**
Roehampton c. 1955 **213**
Rollieflex 23, 150
Rosling, Alfred **39**

Route Ornate, The **125**
Royal Adelaide Gallery of
Practical Science 34
Royal Albert Dock Extension
1913 **94**
Royal Panoptican of Science
and Art 39
Royal Photographic Society 9,
40, 79, 81
Royal Victoria Dock
1917 **110–11**
1966 218, **219**
royalty
Albert, Prince Consort,
photographist to 38
Charles (Prince of Wales) and
Diana, wedding **240–1**
George VI coronation and
funeral 23, **161**
Richard I, statue **53**
Victoria, Queen 42, **83**
rural areas **46**
Russian photographers
Arapoff, Cyril 9, 23, **150–5**,
bib 295

S

Saffron Hill 147, **149**
sailors c. 1953 202, **203**
St. Andrew–by–the–Wardrobe
c. 1870 **55**
St. Bartholomews Place
1877 63, **64**
St. Croix 17, **34–5**
St. Giles WC2 c. 1875 **63**
c. 1877 **67**
St. James's Palace c. 1960 **210**
St. John's Wood c. 1955 **212**
St. Mary Overy's Dock 1881 **70**
St. Pancras Station
c. 1900 86, **87**
c. 1965 **217**
St Paul's Cathedral 1853 **39**

c. 1870 **55**
c. 1909 **97**
1940 **166**
1952 200
salt prints 17, 36, **37**, 41, **45–6**
Sanford, John 17, **60**
schools
Hugh Myddleton 1907 **92**
Scots photographers
Galt, Rev. John 21, **86–88**
Scott, Benjamin 125
Seaborne, Mike 8, 9, 29–30,
278–9, bib 295
Segal, Magda 9, **274–5**, bib 295
Serpentine 1924 **119**
servants c. 1936 156, **158**
Shadbolt, George 17, **46**
Shadow of Light bib 294
ships **42–3**, **61**, **98**,
120, **123–4**, **194**
shoppers c. 1930 **134–5**
shops
Soho 1883, 1690–built **72**
youth culture c. 1950 **199**
Short's Gardens c. 1877 **67**
silver prints **80–1**, **90**, **91**, **92**,
98–9, **102**, **103**,**106**, **107–8**,
113–5, **122–9**, **131–7**,
140–1, **150–9**, **163**,
166–73, **188–201**, **210–14**,
216–20, **223–5**, **228–33**,
242–45, **247–58**, **260–62**,
267–9, **273–6**, **280–1**, **283**
see also modern silver prints
Silvertown explosion 1917
110–111
Sinclair, James **105**
Sloane Square c. 1866 **50**
Smith, Adolphe 19, 67, bib 295
Smith, Edwin 27, **210–14**,
bib 295
Smith, William **41**
Smithfield 1877 **64**

302

Smyth, Norah **106–7**

social documentary photography 9, 19, 21, 23, 27, 29–30, **42–3**, 66, **67–9**, **86–8**, **106–7**, **138–41**, **150–2**, 156, **157–60**, **176–7**, **188**, 190, **191–2**, **196–9**, **207–9**, 218, **219**, **221–2**, 223, **232**, **234–45**, **247**, **258–60**, **262–3**, **266**, **270**, **274–85**

Society for Photographing Relics of Old London 19, 52, 56, 60, 63

Socki, Garanth **259**

Soho

  Chinese New Year celebrations 1976 **246**

  interior, stripper's dressing room 1965 **220**

  shop 1883 **72**

  workshop 1981 **256**

soldiers

  army recruitment 1877 **68**

  leave-taking 1940 **178–9**

  leaving for First World War c. 1915 **112**

  marching c. 1960 **210**

  wounded 1918 **113**

South Kensington Museum 53

Southam Street 1958 **207**

Southwark 52

  1881 **70**

  c. 1930 125, **127**

Southwark Bridge c. 1930 **127**

  1941 **170**

  c. 1972 **229**

Speller, Reggie 119, **183**

Spencer, Terry 27, **224–5**

Spender, Humphrey 23, **138–9**

Spitalfields c. 1900 **86**

  1974–9 **234–7**

  1990s **276**

Spitalfields Market 1973 **232**

c. 1975 **242**

squatters **284–5**

Stamford Hill family 1993 **275**

statues

  Eros at night **233**

  Nelson's Column 36, **37**

  Richard I **53**

Stepney 1940 **180**

  house interior c. 1934 **139**

stereoscope pictures 19, 47, 74, 83

Stone, John H **194**

Stowage c. 1993 **251**

Strand c. 1862 **47**

Street Incidents see Street Life in London

street life 11, 17, 19, 27, **47**, 65–6, **67–8**, **80–2**, 86, **88–9**, **102**, **113**, **118**, **122**, **134–5**, **138**, 140, **141**, **144–5**, **150**, **151**, **176**, **180–2**, **196**, **202–4**, **206**, **207**, **222**, **224–5**, **230**, **238**, 242, **243–6**, **248–50**, **276**, **277**

  see also street traders

Street Life in London 19, bib 295

Street Photographs of Roger Mayne, The bib 294

street traders

  cats' meat man 1902 **88**

  flag seller 1918 **113**

  gypsy horse dealers 1948 **188**

  magazine seller 1893 **81**

  milk cart c. 1935 144, **145**

  newspaper seller c. 1955 **206**

  shoe-black 1952 190, **192**

  windmill seller c. 1935 **149**

  see also markets; street life

Streets of London, The, Vol 1, Westminster bib 295

strikes *see* demonstrations; General Strike

Strudwick, William 17, **52–5**, bib 294

Stuart, Francis G.O. 19, **75**

suburbia c. 1930 **134–5**

  1954 **205**

  c. 1955 **212**

  1969 **225**

  1982 **258**

  1989 **268**

suffragettes **100–101,** 106, bib 294

Sunday newspapers, colour supplements 27, 218, 220, 232, 246, 257, 274

Surrey Commercial Docks

  c. 1876 **65**

  1906 **91**

Suschitzky, Wolfgang 9, **144–6,** bib 295

Sutton High Street c. 1930 **134–5**

swing lens panoramic cameras 19, **89, 264–5, 282**

Swiss photographers **233**

Sygma Photo Agency **257**

T

Tapper, Bob **263**

tattoos **262**

Taylor, John R. J. **258**, bib 295

Temple Bar c. 1862 **47**

Teviot Street c. 1953 **201**

textile sweatshops **235**

Thames, River 21

  1845 Hungerford Bridge 36, 37

  1853 riverfront from London Bridge **39**

  c. 1860 near Westminster **47**

  c. 1862 Eel Pie Island **48**

  c. 1866 riverside houses **52**

  c. 1870 Chelsea riverfront from Battersea Bridge **61**

  1870 Thames bank distillery **62**

  c. 1876 Canada Dock **65**

  c. 1877 riverworkers **69**

  1881 St Mary Overy's Dock **70**

  1885 Limehouse Cut **73**

  1885 Regent's Canal Dock **73**

  1890 Richmond 76, **78**

  1891 pleasureboats **79**

  1895 frozen over **82**

  1896 snow on the Embankment **81**

  1907 Billingsgate pier **98**

  1909 County Hall site **93**

  1909 Wapping **96**

  1909 St Paul's from the river **97**

  1925 Richmond Bridge **120**

  1930 pleasureboats **130**

  c. 1930 at Gravesend **124**

  n.d. Westminster at night **142**

  c. 1935 at Kew Bridge **155**

  c. 1935 industrial scene **142**

  1936 Pool of London 120, **121**

  c. 1937 Embankment, Cleopatra's Needle **163–5**

  c. 1948 Pool of London **194**

  c. 1960 dereliction **214**

  c. 1972 east from Blackfriars **229**

  1979 King George V Dock **252**

Thames from London to Oxford in Forty Photographs 47

theatres

  Old Empire 1895 **80**

Thomson, John 19, 66, **67–9,** bib 295

Tibbs, Fred 25, **170–73,** bib 295

Tony Ray-Jones bib 294

Topical Press **178–9**

topographical photographers 27,

29, 44, 52, 76, 100, **124,
144, 207–9, 234, 254, 258, 260**

Tower of London c. 1930   **12**
  1979   **248**

Trafalgar Square 1839
  1843   36, **37**
  c. 1885   **75**
  1918   **115**
  1923   **118**
  c. 1930   **126**
  c. 1935   **153**
  c. 1975   **245**

traffic   11
  c. 1900   **89**
  1909   **97**
  c. 1913   **105**
  1926   **122**
  c. 1930   **132**
  c. 1936   156, **158**
  see also motor vehicles

Trainer, David   9, **280–81**

travellers
  1948   **188**
  1989   **267**
  1990s   280, **281**

Trevor, Paul   9, 29, **234–7**

Trinity Square
  1913   **94**

Tudor-Hart, Edith   **150**

U

underground railway
  construction of Metropolitan
   District Line
    1865–1868   **50–51**
  passengers   **277**
  station, Oxford Circus
   1994   **280**
  use as shelters in World War II
    167–9

Underwood & Underwood   **83**

Unexplored London   bib 294

University of Westminster   200

V

VE Day celebrations 1945   **185**

Victoria c. 1866   **50–51**

Victoria Bus Station
  c. 1935   144, **145**

Victoria Railway Station
  c. 1960   **215**

Victorian Snapshots   80, bib 294

W

Walworth 1980   **249**

Wapping c. 1909   **96**
  c. 1935   **154**

warehouses
  c. 1906   **91**
  1941 (ablaze)   **182**
  c. 1960   **214**
  1982   **257**

Warwick Lane c. 1870   **60,** 63

Water Gate of York House   52

waterways *see* Lea, River;
  Regent's Canal; Thames, River

Weekly Illustrated   23, 140, 156

West End, demonstration
  through, 1909   **101**

Westminster *see* City of
  Westminster; Palace of
  Westminster

Westminster Abbey c. 1857   **45**
  c. 1877, nearby pub   **68**

wet collodion process   17, 44

wharves c. 1853   **39**
  c. 1960   **214**
  Canary 1991   **269**
  Fresh 1948   **194**
  Greenmoor 1930   **125**
  Hays 1948   **194**
  1985   **254**

Whiffin, William   21, **102,**
    122–3, 201

Whitechapel c. 1938   **138**
  1979   **235**

Whitechapel High Street
  1986   **263**

Whitechapel Road 1981   **255**

Whitehall 1839   **34–5**

Wilson, Charles A.   19, 76, **77–8**

Wilson, George Washington   19,
    76, bib 295

Wimbledon 1968   **223**

women photographers   **150**
  Broom, Christina   **100–101**
  Fear, Sally   **246**
  Fox, Anna   **266**
  Harker, Margaret   **200**
  Matze, Yoke   **260–61**
  Monck, Margaret   23, **147–9**
  Segal, Magda   **274–5**
  Smyth, Norah   **106–7**

Women Photographers   bib 295

Women's Dreadnought   105

'Women's Exhibition & Sale of
  Works in the Colours'   **100–101**

women's suffrage *see* suffragettes

Wonderful London   21, bib 294

Wood Street, City 1990   **253**

Woodburytypes   **67–9**

workhouses c. 1877   **67**

working people
  bargemen c. 1877   **69**
  City businessman c. 1955   **206**
  council employees   **90**
  dockworkers, striking
   1951   **199**
  firefighters 1941   180, **182**
  hatmaker c. 1930   **133**
  labourers Covent Garden
   c. 1877   **69**
  lightermen c. 1877   **69**
  office workers 1987   **266**
  parson 1940   **180**
  rail gang c. 1900   86, **87**
  rescue workers
   1941   180, **181**
  rivermen c. 1877   **69**

roadmenders 1903   **90**

salesmen 1987   **266**

street sweepers 1903   **90**

stripper 1965   **220**

TV crew 1980   **249**

unemployed queuing for work
  1931   **136**

van driver c. 1933   **250**

warehousemen 1906   **91**

women as workers
  1918   113, **114**
  see also policemen; sailors;
   soldiers street traders

workshops c. 1910   **99**
  1979   **235**
  1981   **256**

Workstation   266, bib 294

Wroblewski, Chris   **262**, bib 295

Y

youth
  culture c. 1950   **197**
  Enfield Park 1967   **221**
  homeless, c. 1856   **41**
  hippies, skinheads 1969   **224**
  mods 1969   **225**
  tattooed skinheads 1985   **262**
  'Teds' c. 1972   **230**